Hackers'
tales

This is a Carlton Book

First published in 2004 by
Carlton Books
20 Mortimer Street
London W1T 3JW

ISBN 1-84442-809-5

Typeset by e-type, Liverpool

Printed and bound in Great Britain

10 9 8 7 6 5 4 3 2 1

Hackers' tales

Stories from the electronic front line

Dr K

CARLTON
BOOKS

Disclaimer

This book is intended as a guide to information retrieval, which may help computer security and guard against hackers. The author and publisher expressly do not advocate any activity that could be illegal in any manner. The reader is advised to consult with his or her attorney concerning applicable Federal and State laws. The author and publisher assume no responsibility for any injury and/or damage to persons and property that is incurred as a consequence, directly or indirectly, of the use and application of any of the contents of this work.

Dedication

This book is based on a collection of interviews with, and contributions from, hackers during the year 2003.

I'd like to thank the following people for their assistance in making this book possible:

Zap, Reverend Rat, Lensman, Typhoon, Napalm, Encrypted Error, FreakyClown, Nomad, Zak DeZero, Toxic Foetus, Genocide, Frink, Delta-9, Mark, Rain Forest Puppy, Minus-Q and Summer Elizabeth.

I would also like to thank Alex DeLarge and all the BrumCon crew for their hospitality earlier this year, along with all the London *2600* regulars for such stimulating and interesting conversations.

Finally, I'd like to thank all the anonymous hackers who have made this book possible.

You know who you are, you know what you do, and you know why you do it.

Respect to you all.

Dr K
December 2003

Contents

Editor's note

Writing a book like this is not without its difficulties.

Due to the illegal nature of many of the activities described in the book, many of the hackers are referred to only by the initial letter of their handle.

To make the book easier to read, the editor suggests that you use the military and law enforcement phonetic alphabet and replace the initials with the appropriate callsign.

For reference, here is the phonetic alphabet.

A - Alpha	N - November
B - Bravo	O - Oscar
C - Charlie	P - Papa
D - Delta	Q - Quebec
E - Echo	R - Romeo
F - Foxtrot	S - Sierra
G - Golf	T - Tango
H - Hotel	U - Uniform
I - India	V - Victor
J - Juliet	W - Whiskey
K - Kilo	X - X-ray
L - Lima	Y - Yankee
M - Mike	Z - Zulu

I hope that the necessity of anonymizing the names of the contributors to *Hackers' Tales* does not ruin your enjoyment of this book.

Dr K

Introduction

Forget Computers: Let's Hack![1]

It might come as no surprise to find that for a number of years now I have been thinking about hackers and hacking. However, some of the questions I have been thinking about and some of the tentative conclusions I have arrived at might be surprising.

After many years as a computer enthusiast, followed by several years on the hacker scene, I was lucky enough to write the *Complete Hacker's Handbook*. In the years that have followed, I have been spending my time talking and writing about hackers and wondering:

'What sort of human activity is hacking and how is it best characterized?'

On the surface of it, this looks like a daft question. After all, hackers know who they are, what they do, and why they do it.

Yet even hackers ask this question – sometimes as a rhetorical question, sometimes as an ironic aside and, in their more reflective moments, sometimes even seriously. I have pondered

---

[1] This chapter is a revised and updated version of a talk given at the BrumCon III conference in September 2003.

this question while researching this book and have examined what hackers have in common, what it is that makes hackers tick and how they fit into the wider scheme of things.

Although some investigators might prefer to focus on the technology used by hackers, I am much more interested in the motivation, methodology and process. Why do hackers hack? What do hackers do when they hack? How do they set about hacking something they initially know nothing about?

Black Box Problems

All hacking begins with a problem. When a hacker finds an unknown system, whether a computer operating system, a phone network, 802.11b wireless communications, smart cards or the combination of all those things that go to make up the Internet, the desire to learn and explore is overwhelming.

Initially, the unknown system is a 'black box' system. The hacker knows nothing about the rules that govern the system; in fact, nothing at all about the system, except that it will be governed by rules of some kind or another.

Often, but not always, the rules that govern the system are a computer program. Because the system is rule-based and not random, it doesn't matter what kind of problem the black box system presents.

When a hacker approaches a black box system, the goal is to understand it using exploration and learning and, no matter what kind of system it is, there is a standard set of procedures which anybody who wishes to be a hacker can learn and apply. For me, this is one of the things which define a hacker.

This might seem counter-intuitive because, on the surface, it would appear that the one thing which defines hackers is their use of technology.

But on closer examination you will find that no single technology defines a hacker; even the computer. This is because hackers use multiple technologies and the computer is not a defining feature of being a hacker.

In fact, the types of technology used for hacking are many and varied, and it would appear that no single technology characterizes hacking. Virtually any technological artefact can be hacked, i.e. picked up, played with, improved and made to do useful things. It doesn't even seem to matter whether they are telephones, Furbies, pagers, greeting cards or even computers.

Thus there is no single technology that binds hackers together. There is no single technology that can be said to be universal: not the computer, not the operating system, not the programming language and certainly not the Internet.

Hackers are very attached to their tools, and have preferences. Hackers argue over the best way to do things all the time. Computer 'holy wars' break out regularly among hackers who believe their way is the 'right' way, and therefore the only way. Common arguments of this kind are: text editors (EMACS vs VI), operating systems (FreeBSD vs Linux) and even web browsers (Opera vs Mozilla).

So if technology alone cannot define the activities of a hacker, then what else is there?

Methodology

Certain methods crop up time and time again, no matter what type of black box system is being investigated. This could be said to be a standard hacker methodology.

When a hacker approaches a problem, information can be restricted or unavailable for the black box system, and in this case the hacker can approach the unknown system using certain methodological tools.

- **Research**
  - How can the hacker get the technical references for this?
  - What can the hacker learn from public sources?

- **Trashing**
  - What documentation can the hacker find from private sources?
  - What other information can the hacker find to facilitate later research?

- **Social Engineering**
  - What public information can the hacker find out by asking people?
  - What private information can the hacker find out by asking people while pretending to be someone else?

- **Interception or Tapping**
  - What information can be found by reading material obtained from trashing, or intercepting network traffic?

Once the initial research phase has concluded, a further phase begins. This is where the hacker puts all the information together, adds a large dash of technical ability and then proceeds to explore the unknown system. The hacker will try things out repeatedly and observe the results. This period of experimentation can go on for a long time before the hacker finally gets results and understands the system enough to hack it successfully.

While I was thinking about hacker methodology, I realized that hackers are not the only group of people to use some of these techniques, and that there are others who also use this methodology in their daily life. These people tend to be professional investigators, who use the same, or similar, methodology to find out confidential, potentially embarrassing and secret things about their targets.

These professional investigators tend to be journalists, industrial spies, members of the security services and law enforcement agencies.

Strangely enough, this is a group of people whose members most espouse a dislike for hackers.

Why is this? Even though these people and hackers share many of the same methodologies, many of them are decidedly anti-hacker, on the grounds that the hacker is a menace to the public, a threat to national security or even a criminal.

I, however, have come to the conclusion that it is because, deep down, this group is annoyed that the hackers are playing with big boys' toys. Toys the hackers were never meant to play with. After all, if the techniques used by certain professional investigators to do their work become known about in the public domain, the people whom they are investigating can take precautions against them.

Worse still, if the knowledge is more widespread, people might even turn the tables and use the same investigative techniques against the investigators, nullifying their advantage.

It's this kind of anxiety that leads the federal government of the USA to come down hard against hackers like Bernie S., when it was alleged he was in possession of the radio frequencies used by the US Secret Service.

But, of course, that's not the whole story.

Investigators get annoyed when their 'secret' techniques are widely publicized, and the recent spate of stories about trashing for information has led a distrustful public to fuel a boom in the sales of personal shredders.

Investigators get annoyed when their 'secret' techniques for gathering information, through a casual use of social engineering – or lying, to give it its proper name – become widely publicized such that the public becomes more cautious about giving out personal information, on the Internet, on the phone or even just in casual conversation.

Investigators get annoyed when hackers come along and play with these big boys' toys and then go and fix the ones that are broken. For the investigators, a good toy is an insecure toy. It allows them to invade the privacy of the person they are investigating with relative ease.

If you have the technical knowledge to tap into email, pager, cellular, wi-fi or Bluetooth connections, if you know how to gather information via trashing and social engineering, then you can be an investigator too. Anyone can get the information, and the investigators like it that way.

Then along comes the hacker, picks up a toy, plays with it for a while before finding out that it is fundamentally broken in some way, and promptly proceeds to fix it. Which is all very well for the hacker, because they aspire to technical excellence, to make things work; but for a professional investigator, the last thing they want is systems that work, because it stops them doing their job.

No wonder the professional investigators hate hackers so much. Not only are hackers playing with big boys' toys, not only are they having fun doing it, but they keep finding the best broken toys and mending them.

So maybe journalists and their ilk understand the technology, understand the methodology but fail to understand hackers' motivation. They fail to understand that hackers like to hack for the sheer love of the technology, the pleasure of exploring and playing with the technology for its own sake.

Yet sometimes I think, more cynically, that journalists, security services and law enforcement understand hacker motivation only too well. They understand its playful nature but wilfully mischaracterize hacking because, at the end of the day, it profits them to do so.

Telling people that the world is full of evil hackers is a great way of scaring the pants off Joe Public, selling more newspapers, getting more funding for anti-hacker initiatives and, ultimately, forcing new legislation into existence. It also allows companies to make a fortune out of anti-spam software, email and web filters, anti-virus software and firewalls.

Of course, they're never going to tackle the real problem; buggy and misconfigured software that is insecure out of the box, and which takes more technical expertise to secure properly than the average user ever wishes to learn.

Then the average user is sold firewalls, anti-virus software and email interception software on the one hand, while selling the idea that the Internet is a Wild West full of evil hackers out to steal your credit card details, your life, your children and, for all I know, the family dog and cat.

It's making a lot of money for a lot of people, but it's as if they're breaking one of our legs and then selling us a crutch.

Motivation

While hackers and professional investigators have many methodologies in common, there's one thing which separates them, and that's motivation.

A hacker is motivated by a love of technology, a desire to learn, play and master the technology for its own sake, because it's fun. It's this playful desire, coupled with an intense curiosity, which leads the hacker on, rather than a pay check at the end of the month.

Hackers are motivated by a love of technology and willingness to play for no particular purpose, other than to learn.

This fun aspect of hacking leads to one answer to the question 'What is hacking?'

Hackers do it rather like mountain climbers, 'Because it's

there', rather like BASE jumpers, 'Because I can' and rather like any human being on the face of the planet, 'Because it's fun'.

- 'Because it's there' – Just like a mountain climber.
- 'Because I can' – Technical ability is available.
- 'Because it's fun' – Playing with technology is fun.

Not only that, but the adrenaline rush that the hacker gets off a successful hack means that hacking really can be considered an extreme sport.

Hackers know why they hack. They do it for the fun of it. Once it stops being fun, they soon turn to something else.

Process

So, when we analyze hacker behaviour, it would seem that neither the technology, nor the methodology, is what is most important in characterizing hacking, but the motivation to play with technology for its own sake. This motivation is what leads the hacker on, to keep digging and playing until the problem yields a solution.

We can characterize the hacking process as follows.

1. Problem   – Some kind of 'black box' system.
2. Research   – Hacker methodology.
3. Experimentation – Play with the system using (2) above.
4. Discovery   – A successful hack.
5. New Problem(s)   – Loop to (1).

When you characterize hacking as an activity in this way, it begins to look like yet another human activity: the process of science. This loop of research and experimentation that eventually yields results is a standard scientific methodology.

So maybe it's wrong to characterize hackers as extreme sports enthusiasts; maybe hackers are more like underground scientists.

Not only do hackers share scientific method with scientists, attacking a black box problem with research and experimentation until it yields results, but they also share other features with scientists, for example:

- Hackers have their own specialized technical vocabulary, which they use to discuss hacking.
- Hackers publish their own research papers in peer-moderated journals such as *PHRACK* and *2600*.
- Hackers hold their own scientific conferences, where people give papers and share their latest findings.
- Hackers have websites that are the focus of communities of like-minded researchers, and where they can discuss the theory and practice of hacking.
- Hackers, who normally work alone in a specialized field, can be surprisingly gregarious when they get together.

This last point is surprising until you think about it.

Like a scientist working in a narrow field such as word recognition, there might only be 200 people in the whole world who can actually understand and appreciate a hacker's work.

Small wonder then that when you put 20 or 50 of those people in the same room they talk to each other about the one thing they love most: computers.

Hackers are no more solitary creatures than many other people. It's just that their chosen field, like that of an academic scientist, means that they spend long hours working on abstruse problems until they get a solution.

If hackers are a type of underground scientist, then maybe Einstein should be made an honorary hacker.

Which makes me wonder.

So who should be elected the patron saint of hackers? Saint Turing? Saint Von Neumann? Saint Stallman? Saint Torvalds? Saint Berners-Lee? Or maybe even Saint Bob?

Although we can characterize hacking in many different ways, descriptions of hacking as a technological or methodological activity fall far short of differentiating it from some other human activities, even when these activities share many features in common.

Similarly, descriptive approaches to defining hacking based on motivation and process throw up similarities with activities such as extreme sports or science, but fail to quantify precisely how hacking differs from these activities.

In the case of a hacker exploring the system of rules that is inside the black box problem, it's only amenable to analysis because the behaviour of the system isn't random; it's governed by the program that is inside the computer, because that program is nothing more than a system of rules that happens to be instantiated inside a computer.

But it doesn't *have* to be in a computer program: it could be instantiated in any other system and still follow a set of rules. In fact, any rule-based system will do, and the rules the hacker is hacking don't have to be instantiated inside a computer program: they can be instantiated in any rule-based system, whether it's technological or social.

If it's a rule-based system, then it can be hacked.

A good example of hacking unknown rule-based systems can be seen in the activities of the early pioneers of flight. These flight hackers had no idea that there was a rule-based system, later to be called aeronautics, which governed the process of flying. They proceeded by trial and error until finally, a full century ago, they succeeded in mastering flight.

In a similar vein, the early alchemists had no idea that they were exploring the rule-based system that later came to be called chemistry, while experimenters trying to prove the existence of the ether had no idea that they were exploring a rule-based system that would later be called physics.

This type of activity, of discovery and exploration, is the common factor that brings together hacking and many other forms of social activity.

Hackers are more like underground scientists than anything else.[2]

But whether you characterize hacking as an extreme sport or an underground science, what it's important to remember is that you don't need a computer to hack, because any rule-based system is amenable to being hacked.

Once hackers are no longer restricted to computers, if hackers can hack any rule-based system then we're due to experience some interesting times. There's a whole new world out there and hackers are in one of the best positions to explore it: they have the methodology, they have the technology and they have the patience.

Perhaps now you understand why I say, 'Forget Computers: Let's Hack'.

Dr K
November 2003

---

[2] Anyone who doubts this should check out the work going on at the Experimental Interaction Unit (www.eiu.org). Is this hacking, art or science? Or maybe it's a mixture of all three...

Getting started

Early Days

I've been playing with computers for a long time. The first time I got my hands on a computer was at about the age of four. My dad worked in the computing centre for one of the Big Four banking institutions and he took me to see the mainframe installation.

It was *huge*, and for a four-year-old this was heaven. There were flashing lights, spinning tape drives, even blokes in white coats. It was just like a James Bond movie. I had no idea what it was all about at the time, but it looked like fun, and I went back many times over the next few years.

The first computer I ever owned was a Sinclair Spectrum which I got for Christmas when I was about eight or nine years old. It was a pig to use because of the awful keyboard, but there were BBC machines at school with proper keyboards, and I did most of my actual serious development on those.

I think I first realized I was a hacker when I was about 12 or 13. I think it was when I saw a copy of *The Hacker's Handbook - ZX Spectrum 48K Communications Guide*, but even then, I wasn't *sure* that I was a hacker. Until then, I didn't even know what a hacker was. I was just a kid who was really interested in computers. I knew you could circumvent the security measures on some systems, but I had no specific name for that. I just thought it was something people who knew enough about systems would be able to do, and that the measures were only there to stop the people who didn't.

I'm a terrible geek. I love computers. In our house we have several ZX81s, two Spectrums, a Spectrum +3, an Atari ST, a Tulip AT 286 16Mhz, all sadly gathering dust in cupboards and lofts. There are also two 486 DX50s, one of those awful Amstrad notebook models with the BBC basic in ROM, two laptops, two Athlon machines, a Palm Pilot, a Psion 5MX, a nasty old Pentium box running an IDS and a wireless, ADSL-connected network. My SO[3] is very understanding about this.

I love to program, and I love to program in all sorts of different languages: sometimes I'll write a program in VB or VC++ on my break at work, then come home and rewrite it in PERL to see how much smaller and/or easier to code it is.

Some of the most fun I've had with technology recently has been building, configuring and installing the in-house LAN. It's something I've been meaning to do for years and only just got around to.

I have accessed systems that I wasn't supposed to: sometimes to learn, and sometimes just for fun; and although I currently have no plans to do so again, I wouldn't rule it out, either.

When I realized that I was a hacker, I did what I later learned was the standard thing at the time. I got into communications and BBSs, and hacked Prestel and Micronet over the school phone lines. It was easy then: no one really knew what the modem was for. It was just lying there, not doing much,

---

[3] *Editor's Note*: SO – 'Significant Other'.

and there was no such thing as itemized billing, so no one at the school knew what we were up to. We were able to access Micronet via a premium-rate line, and Prestel – well, *everyone* was in Prestel. I wouldn't be surprised to find that Prestel had fewer legitimate users than it did hackers.

I discovered there were other people out there doing the same things, exploring these new systems. These people called themselves hackers, so that's what I called myself. Once I had that legitimacy of knowing that there were others, I got a bit carried away, and cracked the locks on the IT teacher's drawer and cupboard to obtain software I wasn't supposed to have, which effectively made me the god of the BBC Econet network. That didn't go down especially well, but it was fun.

Probably the most interesting systems in those days (to me) were the Videotext systems. Similar to Prestel, you dialled into a node, selected a service and entered your four-digit ID and four-digit PIN. The world was yours for eight integers: banks, credit records, business data, airline bookings, everything. It never once occurred to me to try to rob the banks, or change the credit data; after all, I didn't even have a bank account of my own then!

I like it when hackers hang out (physically or electronically) and share tales, info, news and humour. Past that, it's all essentially bogus really: it becomes posturing. It's bad enough as it is, living on a planet ruled by gangs of crazed monkeys with nuclear weapons, without hackers getting involved in all the typical macho mammalian status games as well. It was worse in the Eighties and Nineties than it is now, I think. Maybe that's because so many of the participants have grown up, at least in the communications channels I see.

Generally, I don't take it very seriously. For a long time, there was just me. I didn't know any others, and it's not a need I feel deeply. As long as I know they're there, I'm happy. This allows me to live a real life in the real world without worrying what people are saying about me on Usenet, for example. I can always just unplug Usenet; my SO and my family aren't so easy to disconnect!

Computer Exploration

B efore hacking, before using computers and things like that, it was just growing up with exploration. I was always curious as a child and I used to go to school where I lived in Brixton. It used to have an adventure playground in there, so it gave me a sense of adventure and exploration. I'd always come back muddy and stuff. So that's that kind of background.

When I went to secondary school in 1981 I saw my first two computers, a ZX80 and a ZX81, in a maths club that ran at lunchtime. My form tutor was actually the person running it and I saw the potential of computers. I was really interested in arcade machines and used to waste money and time playing those, and I thought 'Hey! A computer! You can learn from it *and* play games.'

A ZX81 is a black-and-white graphics machine with a fairly low resolution. Unfortunately I didn't come from a fairly well-off background, so I had to save up my hard-earned pocket money, and it wasn't until 1983 that I bought my first computer second-hand. It was a 1K ZX81 and I think it cost me £23 ($45). In those days, being a 13-year-old, it was a lot of money – well, it was for me, anyway – but I got some games and programs with it and stuff, and that got me started.

I started collecting computer magazines. Computer magazines were good because they showed you how to do programming and you tended to learn a lot. About that time they had programmes on the BBC about computers with this guy called

Harris or something, and I learnt a lot from that as well. I also used to watch a lot of Open University programmes. I was a very bright child, but in some ways I think I was held back by formal education.

That's how I got into computers. My family background didn't help, because I lost my ZX81 computer when it was shipped to Spain. In 1983–84 *Wargames* came out, and also the original *Hacker's Handbook* by Hugo Cornwall/Peter Sommer, who is now an expert in computer crime law at the London School of Economics. Once that book came out, I could see a bigger playground with bigger computers to start playing around with.

Unfortunately, I didn't have access to a telephone line, so I had to learn how to use different systems without one. I used to go to Woolwich Library, which had a Prestel terminal. You needed to have a serious reason to go on to it, because it was expensive in those days, but there was one good thing about it: the old lady who was the librarian wouldn't punch in the ID and passwords if you were looking over her shoulder, trying to shoulder-surf, but if she'd already started and you wandered back and look over her shoulder she had to continue. That way you'd have enough time to write it down and get the ID and passwords. A great thing about those Prestel terminals was that you could disconnect the terminal and connect it to bulletin boards and stuff like that, until they worked out what you were doing.

Universities were a good place to play around with computers. Schools and colleges didn't have that many computers in those days – I think most schools had the RM Nimbus – so I started specializing in infiltrating places just to use their systems: more exploration, basically. I went down to Greenwich University and walked round trying to find machines that weren't logged off properly. I started looking around the Novell system and trying to learn about how it worked. I bought a lot of magazines and read a lot of books, played around with computers a lot and just tried to learn more.

I first realized I was a hacker in the early 1990s, maybe earlier. I'm not really sure. I mean, calling yourself a hacker after *Wargames*… after all, I wasn't breaking into military computers; I wasn't even breaking into systems that much, apart from university systems, so I couldn't really justify it. It was only later that I realized I liked playing around with technology, and heard something about *2600* magazine and tried to get hold of copies, but couldn't find an outlet for it. Then one day I was walking around Tower Records and happened to see a few issues of *2600* and thought 'Wow! *2600*! I need to get this', and bought a copy. After reading it, I thought maybe I *was* a hacker, and came out of the closet, so to speak.

RAF Brat

Being an RAF brat, running around from base to base and school to school, you had to learn to be invisible. The best way was to learn the local accent so that you could blend in and avoid a kicking. As you start getting older you realize that there's a pecking order and you have to survive. So I used my wits. I learned every single teacher's signature and sold gate passes, early dinner passes and all the rest of it. I sold cigarettes and drawing equipment and anything on the black market. I made enough to hire a couple of minders for a few cigarettes a day to make sure there weren't any potential marauders on my patch. That's a kind of social engineering hacking, but it's also survival. Hacking is survival; in those circumstances, I'd always use hacking to survive.

What I was doing was figuring out the rules which ran the hierarchy – the pecking order – and then circumventing them.

That's a very good example of non-computer-based hacking, social engineering. Also, for me, as far as computer hacking goes, I haven't got a lot to offer because most of the stuff I've done is mental hacking – hacking wetware. I social-engineered my way into jobs left, right and centre when I was a kid to earn more pocket money. I'd chat to stallholders on the local market and befriend them, and when they wanted to go to the toilet I'd offer to look after the stall. The next thing I knew, I'd be working part-time on the stall and had some cash in my pocket. It was a way of wheedling my way in; you needed to do it if you wanted to make money. It was either that or run with the local gangs and thieving for a living, and I'd rather engineer my way in. It's taking on wetware, and that's a form of hacking.

Just like people, organizations work to a fixed format, and once you've learnt the rules of that format it's just a matter of learning the topics involved in that situation. You place yourself on that format, at the level you're mixing in, and once you've learnt the topics you can converse with people. Social engineering is useful in lots of ways.

Learning

I learned PCs in about six months at college; maybe slightly longer. Around the start of September that year I'd saved up enough money from my grant to buy my own PC. I went to a computer show looking for computers and ended up buying two that day. I always seems to do things in twos: maybe it's because I'm a Gemini, I don't know. I bought a cheap XT, which cost me about £300 ($500), but you could see where I wanted to go with it because the first thing I upgraded was the disk drive, to 3.5", and added some joystick ports. As usual, I tried to build a games machine rather than trying to learn about anything. I also bought this cheap PC-compatible clone, not actually a proper PC. It didn't have a keyboard, and it used this weird 'Priority' DOS. I knew the machines at the college Student Union ran the same kind of DOS, so I figured I could copy the DOS disks to get it running, and maybe borrow a keyboard to test it. I wanted to take it apart and figure out how it worked, and this machine was cheap enough to do that: it only cost me £50 ($80). The next time I went to the same computer show I was able to pick up a keyboard for £5 ($8), so I had a system really cheaply, and that was what I used to learn on. I managed to pick up some chips in an old PC and put those chips into the new PC, so I learned how to upgrade the memory. The disks it was using were different from the ones in the Student Union, so to copy the disks I had to learn the DOS commands to format a lower-density system disk, and eventually I managed to get this thing working. I was so pleased that I'd figured out all by myself how to get this computer working.

I spent all that holiday going through all the disks I'd copied: I had loads of stuff – a few games, a word processor like WordStar, lots of stuff like that. A few months later I bought my Amiga and that had a PC emulator with it, so all of a sudden I had three machines which ran DOS variants and that was how I learned about DOS. That was my first experience with PC-type machines, and when I got back to college I was just really good at using plain DOS. DOS even helps me to this day, because we run Win98 at work and whenever you want to fix it you need to step down to DOS, because Win98 just sits on top of DOS.

Build your own

I wrote my first computer program on a Sinclair programmable calculator in 1976, as well as unsuccessful Fortran at school using mark-sense 80-column cards which were sent as a batch run-off to the County Council mainframe and which generated loads of error output. I built my first computer from a kit back in 1977, a Nascom 2. It had 2,000 solder joints and 16Kb of dynamic RAM chips, instead of the originally promised 8Kb of static RAM. In those days I used to read *Byte* magazine and drool over the S100-bus systems that never saw the light of day in the UK, or stuff that was way too expensive for me, e.g. an Apple, or a Tandy TRS-80 or even the BBC Micro.

High school hacker

My life as a hacker started when I joined high school, but even during primary school I was always interested in them. I had an IT lesson and I thought about hackers and how cool it would be to be able to show off in class. I took CLAIT to start with, because I was young and I didn't really know how to use a computer all that well. I surprised myself in CLAIT because I flew through it. That's when I thought, 'What's this computer programming thing I hear about?' so I decided to take up a course in college while still in high school. The course was Visual Basic, and I did Stages 1 and 2 in about two years.

By this time I had learned a bit about hacking, but Phreaking was my strong point. Then, in Year 10, I think, I installed a lot of random Trojans in the school, which earned me the title of 'computer genius'. All it did was get me the coursework, but it nearly got me expelled from high school. Then I started to wonder how it all works. I started to read, someone pointed me in the way of astalavista.box.sk. I found the library there and started my journey.

Pre-school hacker

Well, I've been using computers since the age of four or so – well, that's as young as I remember using one. I remember using an old laptop that only had some old version of DOS on it, and my mother would teach me how to word-process on it. My curiosity from a young age would get me to browse around generally and see what else it could do.

Then I remember using a black-and-white laptop with Win 3.11, which used a docking station to have a colour screen, throughout most of my childhood. When I was bored, which was a lot of the time, I'd just play around with the computer, install random things, whatever I found I could do. Of course, I messed everything up several times, but that's the way you learn.

Still, up to then I didn't think I knew any more about computers than the average Joe. Then I moved to England at the age of 12, and the Internet had just been introduced at my school. It was the first time I had used the Internet, and possibly Win98.

My mother had a laptop from work, which had Win98 and the Internet too, but both school and laptop had restrictions on the Internet, and at school the local settings stopped me also. There was nothing in particular I wanted to get to. It's just that I had ideas and thought I could get round things in certain ways, and took it as a personal challenge: to defeat something they thought couldn't be defeated; to get my freedom.

Coincidentally, a friend from school showed me a little hackish trick on the school computers where you created a shortcut to the school server on your desktop and you would get folders with everyone's usernames, which I thought was really cool. At the same time, as well, a friend from school, J___, was telling me at morning break how he was playing on the MSN gaming zone and he beat this guy, who then tried 'nuking' his PC. I asked him what that was, and how he knew, and he explained to me. At this point I got really interested in finding out how and why this worked, and wanted to try it myself.

A couple of weeks into spending almost every day reading things off the Internet, most of which I didn't understand yet, he came up to me and said, 'You need a handle.' We were going to post on a forum. I don't remember what his nick was before J___, but it was something quite random, and he then randomly came with O___, and I just used it, and since then it stuck.

In a way, I sort of fit the stereotypical hacker personality. I underachieve – I mean I do well, but not as well as I could. I spend – or used to, anyway – excessive amounts of time on the Internet trying things out and reading things. I still would-n't call myself a hacker. I'm in no way as skilled as a proper hacker. Maybe I'm a script kiddie or developed kiddie, but have the brain and logic sometimes to get further the more skilled I get. Also, I consider myself white hat… or white with a few black dots.

The most evil thing I've done is nuke a whole range of IPs because a guy was annoying me, trying to nuke me, and every time I got him disconnected he'd reconnect with a similar IP, so I just decided to hit them all eventually.

I have been attending London *2600* meetings for months, maybe over a year now, and I've set up Egypt *2600* (http://egypt2600.net) recently. I've also had pictures published in the back of *2600* magazine. The website www.totse.com posted a tutorial on hacking email accounts for newbies and they gave it a top rating. I'm 17, by the way.

The first time I went to a *2600* meeting I'd had had no experience in wireless before, and I wasn't used to meeting proper hackers, either. We went to a burger bar in Tottenham Court Road, I think. Then V___ got his 'cantenna' out, which was a converted dog food can, and we sat there leeching Internet connection from the company next door. Then they tried to connect to buses on the road, and a random passer-by who had connectivity on his phone switched on. I was quite impressed by all this at the time, as I hadn't seen wireless hacking in action before.

One time we went to the meeting and we met as usual, and at that time we'd usually go every month up to the sports bar by the bowling alley. Anyway, the group managed to split in two somehow, by accident, and some of us went through a staff door. We got so lost in the insides of the building where we were – it's really huge; you should go in there some day – and we got into a deserted part of the building. We wandered around for ages, trying to avoid cameras and security devices, trying to find a way out, until eventually we found a door, but just as we came out a cleaner came towards us. We just pretended to be lost and he let us out, but he was a little suspicious.

Hacker quest

I would say my first foray into the world of computers was when I was very young, about eight or nine, and progressing very quickly from the early game consoles of that time (Atari 2600, Binatone etc.) and then on to an Amiga 500 when I was at school. My parents ran pubs for a living, which meant that I was given pretty much a free rein to do what I liked. I used to play pool, get free games on the arcade machines, build rockets and bombs, all that kind of thing. It was well before I turned 13 that I was able to pick locks, as well as other 'anti-social' behaviour, but it's worth pointing out that I didn't do much of the social side of life, drinking, smoking or drugs, even though I lived in several pubs where I saw a lot of that kind of thing.

I had, and still have, a huge thirst for knowledge about things I don't know about. To me, school was boring: I found it a waste of time, and that's when I started to get into computers. It was during this period that I realized that computers were in my life for good. I eventually acquired a PC when I was studying science at college. This brought me into the underworld of BBSs and warez. But my thirst for knowledge about just about everything, not just computers, was never – and still isn't – satisfied. The rest, as they say, is history.

It was when I got my Amiga 500 that I knew that there was no turning back for me: endlessly tweaking, chatting, everything was there for me. I could talk to people on the other side of the planet while my schoolmates played soccer, but I knew which I'd rather be doing.

I don't see myself as a hacker – no, really, I don't. I'm an explorer; just someone who wants to know stuff. To me, this quest for knowledge can be compared to a game like Gauntlet: to get the treasure, you need the key. So, too, in life; and if you want the knowledge that's hidden, you have to find the key.

Sometimes it's a physical door, sometimes a person, sometimes a computer password. That's the cool part: you never know what you need, and the effort is way more than the secret you get is worth, but you know you have more knowledge; another tool for next time.

It seems life has the ultimate gameplay and addictiveness that just leaves you wanting more. Maybe the end goal is to pick the lock on the Pearly Gates and fight God with a huge sword or something!

Although I don't consider myself a hacker, many other people do, and I guess that to a point I play up to the media and Hollywood images of hacking, especially like fast cars and… fast cars.

I think we should try and define the word 'hack' first of all. I see it as (ab)using something in a way other than intended; for example, using a shoe for a hammer. But if you are using the media propaganda view of hacking to mean the anti-social use of a computer to gain money, respect or political gain, the first 'evil' thing I ever did was for money, plain and simple.

This is going to sound much better than it was, and much harder than it was too.

I did my work experience at school with a friend of mine called M____. We both managed to land a cushy job doing data entry-type work at a small local bank. It was the kind of badly run place that has about as much security as a wet paper bag. Towards the end of our time there, we were on our lunch break when we noticed a way to get around their signature-checking procedures while withdrawing money over the counter. A month later we walked out of the bank with some cash after nearly emptying some poor guy's account.

I guess I do it because of several reasons. First off, there's the power of knowledge. That's what I'm in it for, and the rarer the knowledge the better. Secondly, it's fun! Finally – to break another media myth – it's really social. People don't realize it, but hackers are a very social bunch. So 99 per cent of hacks are done sitting on your own at the computer; but when we get out, it's always a big social gathering.

As for the morality of it all; for me, denial of knowledge is a much worse crime and there are many things far worse than hacking. To the best of my knowledge, hacking has never killed anyone.

Out of the closet

At this time I thought I was the only hacker in the world: I was just doing what I was doing and thought I was the only one who was doing anything like this. I didn't know anyone else who was doing it. That's what I love, going to the *2600* meetings, because I found a whole load of kindred spirits.

It was about 1993 or 1994 when I first realized that I was a hacker. Those were the golden years of London *2600* because there were some very knowledgeable and intelligent people there. Some of them I would call mentors, like R____. They'd give me information and pointed me in the right direction. I met a guy called Y____ who put me on to Internet Relay Chat (IRC), which I didn't know existed. On IRC I suddenly became immersed in the underground; it was like a common brotherhood where you could trade information.

On IRC there was a free exchange of information, fairly open as long as you got accepted into the scene, and getting accepted wasn't very hard. After you went to a few meetings, everyone would suss out whether you were a hacker, a non-hacker, a lamer, a fed or whatever, and you sort of got accepted. In fact, it was very easy to be accepted in those days. There wasn't so much elitism, and there weren't so many computer crimes reported: it wasn't so bad to be a hacker. These days, it's like hackers are computer criminals, but we weren't: we were just teenagers playing around.

Econet fun

One of the most memorable hacks would be the time I was banned from the computer room at school for being a pain in the ass, causing programs to run on other people's machines, that kind of thing. Those BBCs had built-in speech synths.

I thought at the time that the IT teacher was quite harsh and unreasonable in this matter. I sneaked back in after everyone else had gone home, cracked the system, and removed all privileged access except for my own. Two days later he called me in to see him, and we cut a deal. I was allowed back into the computer room, and he wouldn't have to call an Acorn engineer out to rebuild the system – something that he was totally incapable of doing himself – at vast cost to the school. Also, he wouldn't have to explain to the headmaster that a 12-year-old had shafted him. I was lucky: if he hadn't been so bothered about being made to look stupid, I'm sure I would have been in a world of trouble.

I always remember that hack, because it was a victory of sorts over the people I felt were in charge of all the cool IT stuff, but were basically just in my way. It was also the first time I had put my skills to the test against a real grown-up.

Hacker Ethics

Traditional hacker

I would consider myself a hacker by the traditional definition; but it really does depend on how you define a hacker.

The old hacker ethic, I think, is good, and I have no moral qualms with exploration. I believe the DMCA to be evil incarnate and they will not prevent me from taking everything I have apart 'til they prise it from my cold, dead fingers, to coin a phrase.

Criminal mentality is a whole other arena; one in which I do not participate.

Under recent laws, people – even I – could be branded a criminal for doing (I believe) such things as using a DeCSS DVD player, playing Region n DVDs in my hacked multi-region player, hacking my region's player into a multi-region player etc.

It all depends upon where you get your morals from and what you then do with them. I have what I think is a very well-defined moral landscape.

At the moment I find the whole US scene very interesting. Only the other day I read of somebody being sued for developing and selling a universal garage door opener. The case was thrown out, but the precedent of people suing for ridiculous so-called DMCA infringements is set. I only hope it doesn't make it across the pond.

Another interesting precedent which has been set (again in the US and, to some extent, in the UK too) is that innocent people who have pointed out that such-and-such an organization's network is insecure (say, a 802.11b network with no WEP or anything) are being prosecuted, whereas anybody with any sense would thank them, and even buy them lunch. The problem is that, rather than tell them of their problems, this tends to make people just leave it for some other far more, shall we say, malicious person to do something about.

For the rest of it, I really don't care about SCO because I'll keep on using Linux whatever they do. DRM doesn't affect me as I hardly ever buy music or video, and all this palladium nonsense, well, I'm sure there'll be a way around that too.

So long as I'm still able to proclaim freely the gospel of Jesus Christ I don't care about ID cards, DRM, DMCA or RIP, and when I can't freely do this, I'll do it anyway.

Quite a few people have told me that I am the only Christian hacker they've ever met. I find I've taken a lot over from hacking to being a Christian.

First and foremost, a hacker wants to know how things work. Not being happy just knowing that this box does that and that box does this, a hacker wants to know what happens inside the box, and then why that's so. I want to know what happens inside reality, which drives me to study the world and the Bible to find out why things are so.

Before I was a Christian, I would happily engage in various dubious activities – nothing really illegal (well, not *really* illegal). How does it all fit into my life?

I'm a changed person. When I became a Christian my life

goals, ambitions and motivations changed completely. Where I was once motivated by the pursuit of knowledge, taking things apart and seeing how they work and building a bigger, better and faster network, I'm now motivated by the Gospel and making it known.

Of course, I still like all the above – just at a lower priority!

The biggest change is that where I used to love my job, flying around building networks and fixing things, I now find it pretty boring. Whilst I still get high on new toys and love a good challenge, it simply doesn't hold the appeal it once did.

I've had a few jobs, but usually I'm involved on the IP design/engineering side of building networks. That involves some security, but not as much as I'd like. Usually I just build a network and don't care what runs over it, although things are beginning to get a little more complex now.

Everybody at work knows I go to the meets and nobody cares: I've tried to get to DEFCON on the company, but always had other stuff to do instead.

Apart from computers, I used to be a radio ham, but life got too busy for it and when I moved to London, space got too small. These days, apart from computers, I'm studying theology on a distance-learning course from London Bible College (www.londonbiblecollege.ac.uk), which ideally I'd like to do full-time, and I'm an outreach leader (evangelist) for a London church (Twynholm Baptist Church: www.twynholm.org).

I'm also now married and so have to rationalize my computing infrastructure (one desktop PC, one server and a laptop or two!).

For the future, I want to get my PhD in theology and write some books. I like the LBC motto ('To communicate simply you must understand profoundly') and have found it to be true in the computing world.

Mentors

One of the things I've found useful when getting into the London hacking scene is finding mentors or advisers: people who could point me in the right direction; not necessarily give me the answers, but encourage with suggestions, advice, say, 'Have you thought about this?' and help me think about problems. Certain people like R___ or Y___ have really encouraged me. Y___ gave me an account on a university computer and taught me about Internet Relay Chat (IRC), which I've been addicted to ever since: not just because of the social thing of talking to people, but also because of the 'warez'.

There's a load of stuff on IRC. I find it amusing that Microsoft has closed down its chatrooms, because everyone who's a hacker would use the 'proper' Internet chat, IRC. It's less restricted and there's no policing. With IRC there's more freedom, apart from the channel moderators, so it's much better: it's more underground. When you mention chat programs to people, they always think Yahoo!, MSN, AOL, chatrooms like that; but that's not the proper chat. You can transfer files, you can chat to people, but it's not the proper chat: it's too restricted.

Because I found mentors useful, I've tried to carry on the tradition, and I advised B____ on certain things when he came into the scene. He's done really well for himself: he's totally dropped Microsoft and he's running Open Source software instead, which I find pretty good, considering that I still use Microsoft products because it's quicker to do my day-to-day stuff. I don't really play around with Linux as much as I should; even H___ was having a go at me for not using Open Source software.

At the moment there's a young hacker at the local hacker meetings, and he's just turned 18, but unfortunately his father's dead, so he kind of sees me as a father figure and I try and point him in the right direction. Basically, because I've been active on the hacking scene since 1993 or so, I get treated like some kind of leader. I see a lot of people on IRC who say, 'I want to go to a hacker meeting, but I'd be scared because I'd be too lame', or whatever; so I say to them, 'Come down to the London meeting and ask for me by name.' Once they're there, I'll look after them and introduce them to everyone so they feel comfortable. I tell them to make sure they tell their parents where they're going, and even encourage them to bring their parents along if they need to. We had one guy come down with his Aunty P___. In fact, Aunty P___ was much cooler than the guy who brought her down. I can't remember his name, but I remember Aunty P___. He only came along once and she came a couple of times. She was great fun, a certain age where she was laid-back and just totally cool. I still get email from her from time to time.

So the tradition of mentoring needs to be encouraged. A watchful eye needs to be kept on the younger hackers so they don't mix with the wrong crowd; get involved with criminals, and things like that. It's hard when you're a young hacker. You've got all the technical skills, the attitude, the testosterone, but the boundaries between right and wrong are more fluid, so it's easier to cross the line. It's important to educate young hackers about ethics and morality, otherwise they get into loads of trouble. They need guidance, and I'm happy to help.

Another of my mentors is A___, and he's very good at that: he has a strong sense of ethics and knows his legal stuff, so he's a good adviser. I asked him for some virus code once, and instead of just telling me that viruses were bad, he asked me why I was interested in viruses. Once I explained that I just wanted to understand how they worked and had no intention of writing a virus, he gave me source code, told me about a book that was out and just generally pointed me in the right direction. So I bought a book about viruses and learned how they worked, and A___ helped me do it, but only once he knew that I had no malicious intent.

People forget that the idea of viruses was once a 'good thing'. Computer scientists designed self-propagating programs as a useful tool. It was only when people started to write 'evil' viruses that it got out of hand. Every so often a company or computer scientist comes up with the idea of building a 'good' virus that replicates across a network and seeks out 'bad' viruses and kills them. One of the ideas that I find interesting is the idea of a worm that seeks out security holes and patches them when it finds them. This would be great if you could get it right; otherwise you'd have a repeat of the Internet Worm designed by Robert Morris in 1988.

Flexible ethics

I regard my morals and ethics as flexible in the sense that, for instance, I wouldn't normally kill a baby, but if that baby were the spawn of the Antichrist, sent to surely kill us all, I'd certainly consider it as an option. In the same way, I wouldn't mess with critical infrastructure just for kicks. The recent power failures in London and the States scared me senseless, largely because someone I knew well was in Intensive Care hooked up to a machine at the time. If there were some overriding circumstance – Satanic possession, national crisis, forgot to put nicotine patch on etc. – things would possibly be different.

The location of the line I will not cross is flexible, but largely it's the one chalked on the floor just outside a police cell. I know of people who have, for instance, installed various key loggers and activity trackers to surveil their SOs. I wouldn't do that. I wouldn't read anyone's email just because I could: I don't snoop network traffic at work. There are various reasons for that: partly – and it's a large part – because of the old maxim about eavesdroppers never hearing any good about themselves, partly because I respect most of the people around me enough to not want to play them like that and partly because it's a very slippery road to start down. Before you know it, you'll have everyone you know under surveillance. That kind of paranoia is truly disturbing (NSA, please take note).

On the other hand, if I were penetrating a system I'd want to see the system administrator's email, and if my goal were to steal information I'd want to scan users' mails to find it or any other valuable info. I should probably point out at this point that I'm not engaged in any such activity, and have no intention of being so engaged, so I don't get a knock from our LE friends!

I guess this boils down to what you might call target definition. If I have no particular reason to target someone's personal info, I wouldn't. Even if I did, but that person was someone close to me, I probably wouldn't, because that establishes a very nasty power imbalance in the relationship. People really hate that; it scares them, as it should. Outside of that, I still wouldn't do it for kicks, but if I needed to access someone's personal info as part of a targeted exercise towards some predefined goal, that would be different.

As far as the other line goes – the police cell one: well, why mess up your life?

A long time ago – you'll remember this – a guy called C___, whose name turned up recently, allegedly hacked CurrantBun.com. He did it largely to impress the posters to a

USENET group, but also to get his own back on his ISP. He was arrested, as well as publicly humiliated, and hasn't been heard from since, as far as I know. More recently we saw the trial of Aaron Caffrey[4], who was lucky enough to avoid conviction. He allegedly launched a denial of service (DoS) attack against someone for slagging off his online squeeze. Basically, he's set about screwing his life up with a passion, just because of some scrolling ASCII on a screen, and that seems largely pointless to me.

On the other hand, if I was 70 per cent certain that I could penetrate the systems of Banco del Haxo, fleece them for a few million, get the money out, launder it, access it and get away clean, I'd be prepared to take the risk. This is something that comes up regularly in conversations I've had with various people about the notion of profit-motivated hacking and other forms of crime (yes, I have some odd friends).

The problem is that stealing the cash is the easy part, but getting it laundered is hard, especially if it's a large enough amount to risk spending the best years of your life as a Cat A prisoner in some awful high-security island prison. You'd need to be, as they say, 'connected'.

If you tried this, and did get caught, at least you'd get publicly humiliated as someone who hacked a bank, not someone who *accidentally* DoSd some place between you and your IRC buddies during some juvenile testosterone-fuelled idiocy. When you finally get out of prison, maybe some of the nice men you met inside would be willing to provide employment. Who knows? For me, it's a kind of risk-versus-reward differential. Is the reward worth the risk? Or, more succinctly: if you can't do the time, don't do the crime.

Why have ethics? Having ethics mitigates against the risk of me messing my life up for a largely pointless ego trip. That's the most honest answer I can give.

Trading information

There isn't that much trading of information these days. It's very hard to find out things now. Normally it's not at the main *2600* meetings: you have to break off into these small groups, which are very rare and very cliquey as well, where the serious things are going down or they're playing with certain technology. It depends what you're interested in. It's very hard to break into that, and where before it would be a few months of going to *2600* meetings, then being accepted into these little groups and getting more information and finding people who lived in the same area, now it takes a year or more to get accepted into these groups or find out what people are into. Everyone's very secretive; there have been more crimes reported and more convictions, so people are more or less running scared. Most of the old hacking scene have either grown up or dropped out. It's not the same at all: the scene definitely needs a kick up the ass for the scene to be livened up a bit, but I don't know what.

My current concern is the government's idea for identity cards, which they're trying to phase in in this country. For the law-abiding citizen, it's going to be a pain in the ass, but criminals will always get round technology, so it doesn't really help. It's like the Sky TV security systems where the hackers break the encryption so they can watch free programmes, and then it filters down, and the whole criminal underground finds out about the technology. The next thing you know, someone down at a computer fair or boot sale is making money out of a hacker's hard work. It was the same with the Playstation games, pirate software, chipped phones, Sky boxes and cable boxes.

It's funny when you've got some criminally minded friends and they're telling you about a 'new' technology that you've known about for years and they're just getting in to it so they can make money out of it. But it eventually filters down from the hacker world to the criminal world, and that's normally when it hits the tabloids. It was like cellular phone and pager decoding: that hit the headlines only because MPs were sending unencrypted messages via pagers. Once they realized that anyone could have the technology for decoding pager messages, then it was bad news and a scandal, but hackers have been building pager decoders for years.[5]

Criminals ride on the backs of hackers. We've had criminals turn up at *2600* meetings. We had one guy wanting someone to break into a database for some scam. I told all the hackers there not to have anything to do with this guy, because one place you don't want to mess with is the criminal world. With hackers, you just get deleted files or your web page hacked or something, but in the criminal world they tend to blow off kneecaps. I didn't want any of the people there to get involved in it. Being older than the current generation of hackers, I tend to be like a big brother and look after them and steer them on the right route, because I believe hackers should always have ethics and morals. You can have the Hacker Ethic or Hacker Code or whatever it is, or you can have your own: it doesn't matter, as long as you know the difference between right and wrong and you know there's a line you won't cross.

It's not that you can't use your knowledge for profit. Knowing about computers and growing up meant I had to find work at some point, and I use my hacking skills in my current job as a computer technician. It can be very useful, for example, when

---

[5] *Editor's Note*: I saw my first pager decoder in 1993 at Access All Areas 1. This technology is now so widespread that anyone using a pager must take due consideration of security issues, especially if confidential or sensitive data is being handled.

users have screensaver passwords. One guy at work loves tennis, so when his screensaver kicked in while I was fixing his machine it wasn't too hard to guess that his password was 'tennis'. You could also use this information to access his account, adopting the theory that if he uses 'tennis' for a screen-saver password, then his main password could be 'tennis' or 'Wimbledon', and maybe access his account that way.

I've always thought that the weakest link in anything was the human: that's why I'm a social engineer, because some-times it's easier to hack people rather than computers. One skill I found useful is observation. If you can observe things, then you're 99 per cent of the way there. If you notice that a girl's looking at you, then you know she's interested and you're half way to chatting her up. I love girls. My social engineering skills come in very useful for meeting girls, so bang goes the archetypal image of the hacker as a socially inadequate loner. I love meeting girls and have had loads of girlfriends. I might be a hacker, but I'm still human, still like girls and a social life, still like having fun: it's just that my hacking skills make it easier for me to chat up girls.

Hacker fight

Some time around July 1997, just before Access All Areas 3, it was like 'hackers police their own': a little fracas we had in a cybercafe called W___. We used to hang out in this cybercafe all the time and they were great, even after this incident. One Friday we all went drinking and arrived at this cybercafe. We used to go there every Friday and hang around using the computers until they closed, so F___ was talking to people on IRC and was chatting to them and he managed to piss them off, and so they ran a denial of service against this cybercafe – WinNuke, I think – and destroyed their Internet connection completely. So by the end of the evening F___ didn't want to leave, and I wanted him to go: we'd already caused a lot of grief for W___ and I wanted to be able to come back there. What was funny was that this arsehole O___ had been paid by W___ to secure the entire network against hack attacks, DoS – everything like that. He took money to secure the network, he told them he'd done the job, but you can't secure against a lot of DoS attacks because they use basic TCP/IP specification to mount their attacks, so he ripped them off: he shouldn't have charged them for it.

When the DoS attack nuked their entire network they blamed us for it and tried to kick us out of the cybercafe, and F___ didn't want to go. It fell to me to try and get him out of the cybercafe, and he kicked up a fuss: he had one foot either side of the door and was ranting and raving, 'Do you know who I am? I'm F___ the hacker. I'll hack you up, I'll do this, I'll do that, I'll blow up the world.' I managed to throw him out of W___ and keep the peace, so eventually I calmed him down and dragged him down the road, but he was still really angry. He wanted to go back and just destroy this place; he really had that idea of hacker power. He wanted to mess them up real bad. I dragged him down the road to this alley and tried to calm him down, but he still wanted to go back and destroy the cybercafe network, and eventually he lost it and tried to take a punch at me. Now this is in the middle of London's Soho where there are loads of police. I couldn't let him hit me – it wasn't right – but I was worried about being on the street involved in this argument. Everyone was looking, even F___'s best mate S___, and I couldn't let him hit me, so I used this judo throw to chuck him to the ground. I've been doing martial arts for years and can pretty much look after myself. His mate S___ came up saying, 'Leave my mate alone', and I turned round and said, 'Get rid of this guy before I put him on the ground too.'

I'm not a violent person, but you need to be able to look after yourself, and I'm not going to stand there and be a punchbag for anyone. It all calmed down in the end – the judo throw really surprised him, so you could argue that I hacked F___ in some way. To this day F___ still says he kicked my ass, but I just let it go. I don't care that much about being elite, so who cares about the rumours?

These days we get on fine and talk together and stuff, but I was really upset at the time. We'd got really drunk together one time and I'd walked him back up to Euston Station to make sure he was safe, so I was really surprised when he turned on me, but at the end of the day it's just one of the things that add to the myth: my myth, F___'s myth, whatever. Who cares? It just builds up the myth: he says he kicked my ass, but he looks like a college geek. I don't care about my myth: people can figure out who's telling the truth, so it isn't a problem for me. Some people say he's a jumped-up script kiddie, and some people say he really knows his stuff: basically, what happened is that he got busted for hacking, and he's famous because of that. Does that make you a good hacker or a bad hacker if you get busted? Some say bad and other say good: because you weren't good enough not to get caught, then you aren't a very good hacker. Getting caught's bad, but you always seem to get caught for silly little mistakes.

Currency hacks

When the new decimal currency came in, there was a cross-over period where you could use the old pounds, shillings and pence but also the 'new pence' currency system. During this cross-over period I realized that the old half-penny happened to be an identical size to the new twopence piece, and that telephone boxes happened to take the new twopence piece, so an old halfpenny, now worth roughly one-fifth of the value of a new twopence piece, would fit into the telephone boxes of the time. I romped around everyone I knew collecting the old halfpennies: no one I knew could be bothered to change them or use them because they were worthless. I ended up standing outside the local phone box and selling these old halfpennies for one new penny, each making a very nice profit indeed.

Before the new coins, there was another scam, which involved an old penny piece. You heated it up until it was red-hot and then plunged it into plumber's silver dip, the stuff they use for leading the ends of pipes. Once an old penny piece was silver, it was easy to pass it off as a half-crown or two-shilling piece in a handful of change.

Once decimalization came in, the trick was making lead templates of 50 pence pieces and using them to buy things or get change from vending machines. The lead weighed too much, so you had to drill out the middle. The vendors of coin-operated machines retaliated by having a light sensor to see if the dummy coin was drilled out or not. We responded by filling the middle of the hole with plaster of Paris: it weighed less, and the whole thing now passed the tests. Of course, the vending machine operators changed the system: now they used an electric current to check whether the fake coin was genuine, but we got round that by putting a piece of wire in the plaster, or just covering the whole lead coin in silver paper.

Remember the old wooden cigarette machines which used to be in pubs? You could get the old 10 pence pieces and wrap insulating tape round them to make a roll. Then you used a razor blade to separate each of the 10 pence pieces, and when you got one it looked as if it had a rubber band round it. It made the size of the ten pence the same as a 50 pence piece, so for two 10 pence pieces you could buy a packet of fags. Then they started doing continuity testing on the outside of the coin, so we started using silver paper as the last layer of the roll. Then after that they started trying to get really cunning: they wanted continuity all the way through the coin. Some of these systems now require a correct pure density of the material and actually measure the resistance of the material. Slug detection technology's getting smart: it's evolving as it keeps up with the people who are trying to feed these machine fake coins, so it's like an arms race.

There's a guy I know who's worked out how you could hack £1 coins. Think about it: you look at a £1 coin and if it was made out of the right sort of material, how would you know if it was real or not? There are so many different ones about. Look at the writing on the outside rim of the coin, the Queen's head, the writing on the back: it varies so much, you wouldn't know if it was real or not. So as long as it looked and felt right, no one would question whether it was real or not: they'd just think it was a commemorative edition, Welsh, Scottish or something. It wouldn't be like some of the fake £1 coins, which are really bad: even they get passed on, although they're nothing but lead painted with gold or brass paint. Think what would happen if you made loads of ultra-real £1 coins like that. As long as they looked and felt right, they'd work. You could put Mickey Mouse's head on them and they'd still be accepted, because people rarely look at their money in any detail.

Warez

I don't program much, so I don't crack games. In the old days, with ZX81s and Spectrums, you could just copy the software tape-to-tape, so you didn't need to program. I got into the warez scene when I was running an ftp server on computer at a local college. Local colleges are great, because they have space and bandwidth, so they're excellent places to host a warez site. I actually built a PC and left it at the college in the office of someone I knew who worked there. They kind of knew what I was doing, but turned a blind eye to it. It started off to see how quickly I could get software. Once you've got space and bandwidth you soon get invited to join a warez crew, so I decided to specialize as a porn server, storing porn films on the ftp server. I'd get on IRC and then download porn films and store them on my ftp server for anyone to have. I think I called it *Titanic* because I never knew when it would go down and sink without a trace. The one thing about porn films is that they don't date like new releases; you end up with a huge stock of films to trade.

I'm not really into music, so I've never really downloaded MP3s, but I'm familiar with the technology behind Napster, KaZaA and these different things. It's funny how people always get round restrictions: the RIAA are fighting the trading of MP3s, but new file-sharing programs come out all the time. I think the latest thing now is Bit Torrent, where you get a bit of the file from one site and another bit from another site and so on, until you've got the whole file.

It's a shame, because books, films, software, anything in digital format is now pirated. I even saw a copy of Kevin Mitnick's book in Adobe Acrobat format the other day, and that's a shame, because he was treated really badly. In fact, the only piece of 'hacktivism' that I've ever done was to protest outside the American Embassy about Kevin Mitnick's imprisonment. It shocked me that nobody in the UK was going to do anything, and I thought the only way to get something done was to organize a protest myself, so I did. There were only a few people who turned up from the protest: M___ was there, and a couple of others, and a few passers-by who understood what Kevin Mitnick was up against.

I'd spoken to Kevin Mitnick in 1997, and he was convinced

that cellular source code was available on the net: then O___ told him that he 'had some on an encrypted drive some-where'. This annoyed me, because O___'s a complete bull-shitter, and I had to tell Kevin gently that O___ was talking rubbish. So the only thing I could do was to protest about Kevin's imprisonment. I did a website at a local university and wrote up a press release and sent it to NTK[6]. They liked it and published it, but someone spotted where it had come from and reported to the university that they had a hacker there.

The warez scene would go away if software prices came down. I've always thought that if software were cheaper, more people would pay for it; they want a real copy rather than an illegal copy. I've got a real problem with the idea of selling warez: I've thought about it as a quick way of making money, but I can't do it; it's morally wrong. People in the scene are quite happy to trade warez for other warez – you get some-thing back in exchange – but ordinary people will just ask if you've got a copy of Photoshop, say, and if you have, then they just want it. They don't think about the cost in time and the blank CD – sometimes they don't even buy you a drink – but these are the people who benefit from warez and they're riding on the back of the warez scene. Fellow-workers, espe-cially secretaries, are always on my case to get hold of films like *Spiderman*, but they just take it for granted. They don't appreciate it: they just want something for nothing, and at the end of the day, they're taking the mickey.

Hacker wars

I've been involved in a few hacker wars in the past: one that comes to mind is when I was up against my brother and he

---

[6] *Editor's note*: Need To Know – www.ntk.net

locked me out of my sister's university account. Seeing as I was the one who started him off in the hacking scene, though, I knew a little bit more than him, so I created an '.rhosts' file so I could just log back in at any time. The other thing was that when they did change the password I already had root access, so every time they changed the password I just changed it back. That was a funny period, playing hacker wars with my brother.

Other hackers can be real assholes at times. O___ caused a lot of trouble on the scene and I had to mediate between the different groups who were involved. People were playing around with phone lines, redirecting them, all sorts of stuff. Sometimes hackers can be really vindictive just because they have the power. Allegedly, they were blocking people's mobile phones, removing their credit, redirecting phones; all sorts of annoying things like that.

Phreaking ethics

I'm opposed to crime and I'm opposed to profiting from my hacking skills except in the obvious way, when I'm hired to use those skills in an honest way. Once I'm being paid to look after someone's computers, then when I work for them they get a full service – the full monty. When I discovered an insecure phone line in a company, all I could do was secure it for them: that's what I get paid for. I couldn't do credit card fraud because it would be theft, even if it was just the insurance company that was being burned. I don't like all this free phonecall hacking when it's just profit-based. I've played around with plenty of Country Direct numbers looking for C5 exchanges, but I didn't do it for the free phonecalls: I did it to learn about C5 signalling systems. Once hackers start boxing free calls just to call American sex lines because they can, and when they rack up huge bills for people, then I get worried about the ethics of what's happening. I'm really not interested in crime for crime's sake, but sometimes I might break the law a little during my exploration. It's just knowing where to draw the line.

Minor tip

J ust a minor tip for those reading this book.

Firstly, if you can afford it in both time and money, have your network or application penetration-tested. Ask around companies within the same business sector as yourself: ask your IT guys to see if they know of any especially good or bad companies, but do get a third party to take a look at your security and see what holes they can find.

You may think you don't need to do this if you've had the security of your set-up assisted by another company but, even so, it helps to have a different company, with a different mindset, different knowledge and different techniques come in and check what they've done. Also, the security industry is a very incestuous place: the chances are that the company which set up your defence are old friends or rivals of the company which will be testing those defences, which usually spurs them on to greater efforts – all meaning that you'll get more for your money.

Criminal mind?

I keep thinking I have a criminal mind. I see ways of breaking the system, ways around problems, new solutions. I've also got a few friends in the criminal underground, and sometimes it seems there's an intersection of the two worlds. A friend of mine called R___ isn't actually a hacker, but he's learnt how to hack cable TV boxes and he sells them. He guarantees them for life, saying they'll always work, and that's morally and ethically dubious. He wanted me to help him sell these hacked boxes, but I refused: it didn't seem right. Someone else was asking about the digital mileage systems in cars: apparently the new digital ones can be rolled back, so you can hack cars, but in the end the loser's Joe Public: they get ripped off and hackers get a bad name, so once again I refused to get involved. The first guy who ever hacked cable boxes to get free channels was a hacker. He was the first one: he figured it out, but once it filters down to criminals then it's not hacking any more.

Car hacking

Have you heard about these guys who are hacking cars? These days, the performance of a lot of engines is less to do with the engine and more to do with the software which runs it. So these car mechanic guys get high-performance cars and get the EPROM out of the engine management system and an EPROM emulator and then they poke random variables into the EPROM emulator. They run the engine and look at active memory areas, seek out the variables in the code, and when they find a set of parameters which make the engine perform better, they change these variables Then they blow a new EPROM. This is how they get these 180mph road cars, boosting the performance by hacking the EPROM controlling the engine management software. When I first heard about this, I thought they'd be getting a software engineer to decompile the engine management software and figure out what to change that way, but they just do it by trial and error. I was really impressed: there's me, thinking like a properly techie hacker, but these guys are car mechanics, not hackers, so they do it totally differently – yet the end result is the same.

Hacktivism

I like to stand up for hackers' rights; I try to promote hackers in a good light. That's why I've got the reputation of being a media whore. Because I *am* a media whore I've been in a few newspapers, I've been in a few radio broadcasts, I've been on satellite TV a couple of times and mentioned in books. That's a kind of infamy or fame, depending how you look at it, but I've had my fifteen minutes'-worth. There was the case against *2600* having the link to the DeCSS code on its website, and I was outside the court in America just after H2K, sometime in July 2000, protesting about American civil rights and freedom of speech. It was ruled that computer code isn't a language, so the American laws on freedom of speech don't cover it. I found it really funny that someone from Europe, a foreigner, was there standing up for the civil rights of Americans in America. It affects me, though, because the DMCA is being brought into Europe through the WIPO treaties. They actually threw out the case, and it asserted people's rights to do what they want with DVDs which have been purchased legitimately, to play them on whatever platform you like, even though it's an open source operating system. What's going to be scary in the future is if Microsoft gets its Paladin Digital Rights Management system worked out: then everything will be have to done under DRM, and some things we can do now won't be possible.

A musician I know is concerned that the new DRM systems will force their way into music, and that the law will insist on DRM for all digital content, so he'll be in a situation where he won't be able to distribute music in a digital format because he can't afford or doesn't want to use DRM. Why should he? It's his to keep or give away as he wants, but he doesn't want Microsoft to have any control over his music, nor the DMCA, nor anyone else. It's like the SCO case, where SCO UNIX alleges that IBM has stolen its code and put it into Linux. I think that this is just a spoiler tactic by SCO, because it just doesn't make sense. I've used SCO UNIX and I thought it was rubbish, and I've used Linux and it's good. So excuse me if I don't believe that there's SCO code in Linux: it just doesn't make sense. SCO were the market leaders in selling x86 Unix code, and when Linux came along the market evaporated, but the market evaporated long before IBM took any interest in Linux. I believe this is part of a concerted attack on the Gnu Public Licence (GPL), which governs the distribution of source code, and that big business wants to smash the GPL and the open source movement because it sees it as a threat. If big business can discredit Linux, then certain companies will have an open field.

I developed in a different way from most hackers. Not having a telephone line meant that I had to specialize in social engineering and infiltration hacking. I would go onsite to places, I'd dress the part and speak the jargon, and this is why I see myself a bit like the UK's Kevin Mitnick. I obviously haven't got up to exploits like his, or generated a myth like his, but I think I'm like a Kevin Mitnick in training.

Hacker power

Being a hacker, sometimes you don't understand the power you hold. Once I was at college and got kicked off the course because I was telling someone about a proof of concept and how they could insert a virus into the Nimbus system, but the whole proof of concept was actually based around an *AirWolf* episode called 'Moffat's Ghost'. This was stupid. Although this was a concept, no one had done it, but because the episode was about a virus, when they heard about me talking about it and knew that I was a hacker, some teacher or lecturer who heard us talking about it thought it was *real*, and I got barred from the computer system.

The idea of me being a hacker scared them so much they wouldn't let me anywhere a computer: it was as if I was carrying a bomb, or something. I couldn't believe it. It was all based on an overheard discussion about a TV series and they couldn't tell the difference between fact and fiction. It wouldn't have been so bad, but they were so stupid they believed what they wanted to believe, and that caused me loads of shit.

The actual episode relied on a virus which was already in place and would mess up the computers at a later date, and they were so stupid that they stopped me from using the computers at all. I wasn't allowed to touch any of the computers at college. They believed it: but that's a weird kind of hacker power. In the end, I managed to get back on the course on a technicality because I used my social engineering skills. I tend to fight the system because I'm a social engineer, but I shouldn't have had to fight the system in the first place. The lecturers were being really dumb and reacting in a knee-jerk way, even though I hadn't done anything wrong.

Cautionary tale

Once upon a time when I was young – and, as it will transpire, fairly stupid – I worked at a place which was a hangout for various criminals and ne'er-do-wells. It was the kind of place where, if your friend's car stereo had been stolen, you could probably have a word with a punter and get it back. Certain people who had an interest in the place were what we'll call, for want of a better word, 'connected' to what I can only describe as a large organized crime group. They were one of several in the region competing for the various turfs which were to be had – drugs, prostitution etc.

Being young, and stupid, and convinced of my ability to handle myself, I hung about with some of these people, did small favours for them and so on. At this point, I have to stop and point out that although this sounds awfully like some kind of *Goodfellas* rerun, this really is the way it works.

One day, I took a job from someone. He was a private investigator who, on reflection, had absolutely no reason to be talking to me, and he asked me to try to recover records from a PC which had been obtained from a liquidated company. He told me it was suspected that the proprietors of this company had ripped off the money and fled, and he had been hired by their creditors, happened to know my employer and heard that I might be able to help him. Which I did.

I was also handsomely paid, considering that the drive had been formatted and then left alone and the recovery of all the data on it was fairly straightforward.

Later, I found out that the private investigator was working for the aforementioned criminal gang, that the company had been a front for various criminal activities, including money-laundering, and that the proprietors really had nicked the money and run.

Later still, fairly bad, violent things happened to them. I read about it in the newspapers and tiny alarm bells began to ring in my head: not loud enough, though.

Not so long afterwards, I was in some god-awful hole of a nightclub with a couple of lovely ladies and a guy I'd known distantly at school. It turned out that he was not only a 'member', or whatever the hell you want to call it, but also knew I was distantly connected to the organization. We subsequently spent much of the night discussing the idea of various hack-related crimes which might net a profit.

Now, at the time, in my poor little head, I was thinking: 'Well, hey! Here's this club, and these very lovely ladies, and this guy I know a bit who obviously has money to throw around because the drinks are 20-odd pounds each, and he's talking to me about basically becoming a fully paid-up criminal.' Paid being the word. So off I go about my business with a renewed enthusiasm, feeling sure that, before long, I would be hacking shit for what basically amounts to the largest criminal gang in the city. What could be better? What could be worse?

At about this time, unbeknown to me, the turf wars were hotting up. All across the city people were dying of gunshot wounds. Had I made the connection yet? No. It took one final incident for me to realize just exactly what I was getting into.

One night, my friends and I were hanging out in this crap karaoke bar because one of them was a hardcore karaoke fan. We were supposed to meet a guy regarding some bar work and suchlike at a new, criminal-owned club.

He never showed: and the next day, we found out why. Two barrels of a shotgun through the window of your car at short range is generally enough to put a crimp in anyone's schedule. The same night, his new club burned to the ground. Turns out that this guy had stepped on the wrong toe, or something. Although he was connected, he got too big for his boots, and at that point these guys were executing a policy of simply offing anyone who got in their face. Knowing we had been dealing with this scary guy who had just been assassinated, basically, by some other scary guys we knew was something of a wake-up call for all of us, but me in particular, since I was the only one attempting to solicit work from them independently.

From that point onwards I was terrified almost constantly, which meant that I was actually paying attention for a change. As time passed, my employers got more and more involved with the scary criminals, and I had an excellent opportunity to study the criminal culture up close and personal. It wasn't nice at all, not even a bit, not even in a high-adrenaline kind of way.

You see, the problem is that just knowing these people, knowing who they are, knowing what they do and knowing where the money goes puts you in danger. How much do you think these guys will hesitate before killing anyone who is a risk to them? Not long: probably not even long enough to make a decent plan.

Not wishing to die in a hail of hot lead, I worked hard to make sure that any favours which occurred went the right way, from me to them, and that I never knowingly did anything which could carry a prison sentence. The reasons for this are twofold. Firstly, any favours done for you will be recalled later, and you don't get to choose: you just owe them. That gives them control, and that is not a good thing. Secondly, and very similar: once you do a job for them which puts you on the wrong side of the law, your ass belongs to them. This is a movie cliché, but that doesn't stop it from being true. They will *always* have that hold over you, knowing they can drop you in it at any time it suits their purposes.

You think this works both ways just because you know their names and faces as well. Not so: if you turn up at your local police station and rat them out, sure, maybe some of them might do some time, but you'll be dead in a ditch somewhere. To my mind, that's most definitely a non-optimal outcome.

Fortunately for me, around this time I had the opportunity to leave the area and move away, and I did so. I went a *long* way away and tried very hard indeed to forget these people ever existed; and whenever I have cause to think about them, I hope most desperately that they have forgotten me.

I'm sure they have: there are always plenty of hangers-on for them to use up.

So the moral of this story, if there is one at all, is simple: proper criminals are very, very bad people. When you sit in your hacker lair, wishing you could hook up with someone who could launder that two million you always planned to steal from an online bank, just remember this story. Remember that the criminal fraternity and hacking are so far apart, you might as well be an alien from space. They will *not* respect you, they will *not* nurture you and they will not be intellectually stimulating, unless you consider being terrified for 24 hours a day intellectually stimulating.

Being a hardcore criminal is about being an animal; being a hacker is about being a human being. Chalk, meet cheese.

Paranoia

Missing key logger

When you buy a hardware key logger you're meant to give them your name, and they're even quite illegal to own in some countries. Well, V___ managed to blag one from a computer show, and sold it to me. I thought, 'I'll have some fun with this.' It plugs in between the keyboard and the computer and it has 64K of memory. Because it's hardware, it doesn't show up on the task list or anything, and when you type in a certain word anywhere on the computer the menu will pop up.

So off I go to school, to the sixth-form house which is only for sixth-formers, so the computers never get touched there and the admin almost never comes over. I go over there, install it, test it and it works fine, so I wander off. I come back at lunchtime for a quick check to see what's going on, and as I walk in I notice that there are new computers, and think, 'I didn't notice those earlier.' I look round the back of the computers and the keylogger isn't there.

There are four new computers in there and there should be four old ones, but there are *only three*. The whole of the next week I'm really paranoid, thinking that they're finger-printing it and stuff, and worrying about whether the pass-word was strong enough to withstand guessing. One of the boarders comes up to me and says, 'By the way, the IT Admin asked me who the best hacker in the sixth form was', because it's only sixth-formers who use it and there are only a hundred of us. He knows who the hacker was and I know he knows and he knows I know, but we don't say anything: we walk past each other and just smile at each other. I hid the manual in my mate's room because I thought, 'What happens if they search *my* house?'

My mate tells me that my name was mentioned, and then I act normal and calm and just say, 'Cheers for telling me', but I always get the blame for everything from now on. I didn't even get my key logger back: one day I went into the computer room and started checking a pile of computer keyboards and I was close to finishing them all, but then the systems administrator came in and I never found it. I was worried that at parents' evening he was just going to whip it out of his pocket and say, 'Do you know what this is?' right in front of my parents. I was so worried that I might not act calm and normal, I even acted out the scenario with my mate so that I responded calmly. Anyway, at the end of school, when I'm, leaving I plan to go and say, 'Can I have my key logger back, please?'

Paranoid android

When I used to hack regularly, I was really paranoid. I don't mean slightly paranoid; I mean seriously, deeply paranoid. I was so involved with the hacking scene that I was up to my eyeballs in computers and manuals. I was trashing regularly and had documents from trashing runs lying all over the place. I was also Phreaking C5, so I had all the extra fears about Telco investigators. Every time someone had a fault on one of their phones and a Telco van appeared I'd break out into a cold sweat, and if I actually saw an engineer at the top of a pole in my street or, worse still, working on one of the local Telco cabinets, I'd feel physically sick.

The whole thing came to a head when some people I was hanging out with in cyberspace got busted. One guy used to run a BBS and it was rumoured that the police had been tapping the line and tracing all the calls for months to see who else was involved with this hacking group. I packed up everything I thought was incriminating and got a friend with a car to collect it and take it to his place where it would be safe. He only had a little compact model and we filled the trunk and all the back seat with computers, Telco manuals, print-outs, bags of trash, laptops, Phreaking devices and loads of other really dodgy stuff. I left it all at his for months and months before I felt safe enough to collect it.

Although I didn't get busted, I never felt safe hacking after that: the huge scare and ongoing paranoia was way too much for me and I dropped out of the scene. The worst part about it is that some years later, when I changed a carpet in one of the rooms, I found loads of printout stashed underneath the carpet where I'd hidden it. It was full of names and IP addresses of systems I'd compromised and lots of userids and passwords where I'd run the password files through Crack. It was really funny, in a way, because after all the trouble I'd gone to trying to clean up my house, I'd managed to forget the most incriminating evidence of all. Now that I've given up hacking, I'm not so paranoid, but I still believe in the old saying: just because you're paranoid doesn't mean that they're not out to get you.

Home hacking

A couple of years ago, when I was about 13, I was just getting to know the web from school, because we didn't have Internet at home. The only way I could access the Internet from home was to use my mother's laptop, and because it was her work laptop it had Internet filters on it, so I couldn't really get to the sites I wanted to. At the time, I didn't know enough to get round it, but at school the filter was rubbish, so I used the school Internet a lot more.

Anyway, a friend called J___ was the first person to teach me about how nukes and NukeNabber worked. He told me about how this guy on the MSN gaming zone was nuking him and how NukeNabber was just going mad. When I heard this, it got me really interested, so that night I went on the Internet and looked up a load of stuff. I got these lame programs – Trojans and nukes, that kind of stuff. I zipped up the more interesting stuff and tried to send it to J___ . It wasn't anything really dangerous: I just wanted him to check out these programs.

My email wouldn't work – the attachment button wouldn't work – so I asked my mother if I could use her email, but what I didn't realize is that that a copy of everything she sends gets saved in Sent Messages. While doing the email, I get all these virus warnings, and because I know why I'm getting them I just keep pressing Ignore.

The next day my mother comes home from work. Because she had a copy of the message which had the main virus warning, she told her manager in the London office, and he went and told his manager in New York. They ended up updating every computer in every machine in every branch in the world, all because of this anti-virus warning that was caused by me sending some software across to my friend.

She gave me the telling-off of my life. She told me, 'I never want to hear of you doing any of this hacking again', and really went mental. Worse still, when she came in the house I was showing my grandmother the computer with a nuke program that said quite clearly, 'Click here to mess someone's computer up.' I thought it was funny, but she didn't.

I kept a low profile for a few weeks, but in the end my curiosity and thirst for knowledge got the better of me. I went back to doing the same stuff, but I tried to learn from my mistakes. I couldn't care less.

Red-handed

I've been busted various times at school. Once, while I was at university, I discovered my account was locked after the summer break. Naturally this concerned me, since I had a pretty good idea why.

I went to see the appropriate people to find out why, and it turned out that they had discovered a small C program in my home directory. It was the old getpwent.c deshadowing exploit, in fact.

Not wishing to bend over straight away, I suggested that since we'd just been on Christmas break, maybe someone else had hacked into my account while I was absent. Couldn't they check the access logs and find out if someone had dialled in?

I reckoned I was on pretty safe ground here, since there was no way for them to verify that it was me if there were dial-ins from off campus – which, of course, there were.

As it turned out, they couldn't, because they'd purged them and they apparently didn't keep backups. They re-enabled my account while I stood there in the room, although they clearly didn't buy my story at all. The funniest thing was that they kept assuring me that the program would never have worked. They should have been right, but they were dead wrong: this was a Solaris system, and in fact was vulnerable to a race condition of some kind (IIRC). Really, the fact that the deshadowed password file was sitting there in my home directory along with the program should have been a clue.

They didn't even erase the files.

Hard-drive torture

We got very paranoid about what could happen to us if we were caught; besides encrypting our drives, we were worried because the new RIP act states that the maximum sentence for not passing over encryption keys is two years. Now, if your hard drive contains illegal software or that sort of thing, then two years might seem like a nice sentence; but we didn't want to serve two years in jail, so we developed a plan. We went to a computer fair and bought some removable hard-drive caddies so that when the police come and smash the door down you have about 10 seconds to pull the drive out and chuck it out of the window into a neighbour's garden.

Anyway, A___ came up with the best way to crack encryption. I said to him, 'I'm using PGP disk to encrypt my drives and I want something better', and he said, 'There's no point in having encrypted drives.' I was puzzled, and asked him why that was. He replied that he had found the best way to decrypt encrypted drives. If you get arrested, the police can crack the encryption in less than 24 hours. To start with, they'll sit you on a chair and ask you what the encryption keys are.

So you say, 'I've forgotten the encryption keys; I can't even access my own files.'

Within 10 to 15 minutes of you telling them you'e 'forgotten the encryption keys', they come back into the room with a little square box with two electrodes, pull down your trousers and hook the electrodes on to your testicles. Within about minus 15 seconds, you will remember the 'forgotten' keys.

So forget about cracking encryption: electrodes to the testicles are much quicker.

Busted! A hacker's diary

Wednesday, July 2, 2003

M s Smith was asked to return a computer on loan to her by ExCompany.

On Wednesday night I was approached by Ms Smith as a friend and the head of IT of ExCompany to remove any personal items of hers from the PC and get the machine back to a working state. I arranged for this to take place on the Thursday as the PC was due back on the Friday.

Thursday, July 3

I arrived at Ms Smith's house after work and proceeded to remove any personal items she had left on the computer. However, in my opinion the PC was not running perfectly. It was at this point that I, as systems administrator for ExCompany, decided it would be best to reinstall the operating system (Windows 2000 in this case). I hadn't taken into account the time, and that I would not be able to install additional software or drivers. I decided to install all additional software and drivers to meet the boss Mr G___'s requirements for the new function of the machine the next day. At this point the system had a basic Windows 2000 installation ready for customization as required.

Friday, July 4

About 5pm Mr G___ stormed into my office and accused me of ruining the PC on loan to Ms Smith, telling me that I had 'no f*cking right to touch that PC'. This shocked me. I attempted to explain what I had done and that the PC was not unusable, as he alleged: this further enraged Mr G___ who then stormed off.

At approximately 5.30pm he returned, still angry and with no apology for his behaviour earlier, claiming I had damaged the PC and that it would take ages for him to fix. I then provided Mr G___ with CDs which I believed to contain the necessary additional software. He took these and stormed out again.

At approximately 5.40pm, Ms Smith and Mr Other came in to say they were leaving for the day. At this point I had made my decision to leave the company, because of the treatment I had received that day and also similar treatment over the previous few months. I then gave my office keys to Ms Smith in the presences of Mr Other, both of who can attest to my having been sworn at earlier that day.

I then decided to clean out my desk of personal belongings, made sure there was an up-to-date list of passwords required for all machines and uninstalled all my personal items from my desktop machine, which were assorted publicly available tools used for sys-admin work. This PC was otherwise left as it was.

I then went to leave the office and realized that, as I was last out, I did not have any keys to lock up with. I called Ms Smith to come back and lock up for me: this took approximately five to ten minutes. I would estimate the time to be around 5.50pm or 5.55pm. I then left and joined the people from AnotherCompany at the local pub a little before 6pm.

Saturday, July 5

I decided that I should cover myself – because I knew how Mr G___ would react to my quitting – by getting hold of our American developer, Ms America. I then spent a good hour or so with her online talking her through how to shut off my account and change the administrative passwords, as well as other accounts for which I knew the passwords. This action prevented me from remotely accessing the computer network at ExCompany. The ability to disable my accounts also shows that the computer network was functioning, as I have previously stated.

I spent the rest of this day chatting to people online and playing online games. I also spent some time looking online for a new job as well as sending Mr G___ my resignation letter.

Sunday, July 6

I woke up about 11am and spent most of the day job-hunting and chatting online. In the evening I went mountain biking with a friend in Guildford, returning home about 10pm.

Monday, July 7

I received an acceptance letter from Mr G___ regarding my resignation. He claimed I had damaged the computer network and that he was planning legal action.

I then had a request from Ms America for some help: I spent a few hours helping her sort out some minor problems Mr G___ had, although he didn't know I was helping her fix his problems.

Tuesday, July 8

Job-hunting all day.

Wednesday, July 9

I learned that AnotherCompany had been called in by Mr G___ to 'fix' the damage of which I was accused. They stated that they didn't believe any malicious damage had been caused and the only issues with the system were within the normal bounds of running a computer system on the scale of ExCompany. My desktop PC was functional and not unusable, as claimed by Mr G___. The database that Mr G___ said was damaged was also functioning, as was observed by Ms America and anyone who cared to look at the ExCompany website, which relies on that database to be present and working.

Thursday, July 10

Got legal advice from the Citizens' Advice Bureau in Guildford, I informed them of the facts in the case and they were reassuring in that Mr G___ has no case.

Friday, July 11

I received a call from a friend telling me that a police officer had requested my contact details from him and that I should expect his call. At approximately 3.45pm a constable contacted me and we arranged to meet on the Saturday at 2pm at Alton Police Station, which is a 30-mile-plus round-trip for me.

Saturday, July 12

I arrived at the police station for an interview and was told that another constable has taken over the case. They told me that I would be arrested before they could talk to me, and I was then advised to leave and return with a lawyer.

A few days later I returned with my lawyer and was arrested under Section Three of the Computer Misuse Act (CMA). During the booking-in procedure it became evident that they did not have the crime I was being arrested for on their computer systems. They put me down as something else with notes on what it really was. For some reason, this worried me. We then had a two-hour interview on tape, and I was released on bail and told I must return at the end of August to find out if they would continue the case or drop it.

When I turned up with my lawyer in August I was told they hadn't figured out whether they had a case or not and that I would be rebailed until October 19. Right now, I'm waiting for the 19th to find out which way we are to proceed.

As you can see, this has taken the police a horrendous amount of time from August 12 to October 6, and I think it's pretty clear that there's more than reasonable doubt that I have done anything. Maybe the CMA is just a bit too vague and not a lot of the police force know enough about computers to follow it.

I think it's pathetic that just on the word of someone, without any kind of formal investigation, an innocent person can be arrested and thrown into the world of 'red tape' I'm now engulfed in. I've no money because I left my job because my boss wasn't nice and I can't get a job because being on bail for 'computer crime' seriously kills any chance I might have. I've already been turned down for a few because of this fact.

Editor's Note: Subsequent to the writing of this diary, the police charges were dropped. The hacker who contributed this tale is now back at work as a systems administrator and keeping a low profile. It could have been much worse.

Rubber ducky

I remember being at school on the last day of term: we were waiting for the bus. I was blocking a load of junk mail porn someone had signed me up for. I didn't realize the systems administrator could watch what I was doing: I knew he was in his office and just thought he was working. I was sitting next to J___, who was looking up Trojans and port-scanners but not even downloading them or anything, so it wasn't against the school rules. When these younger students came up and stood behind us we even minimized the screens, trying not to attract attention to ourselves.

When they wandered off, we logged off the computers and headed off to get the bus. The systems administrator came up to us and said: 'You might find you're unable to log into the system when you return next term'. So J____ and myself were really scared: we'd never been confronted before. He pointed out that we had signed the acceptable use policy at the start of the year, and I tried to point out that we hadn't downloaded anything from the Internet and that we were just reading. He then accused us of teaching the younger kids behind us, and then dropped his bombshell:'I've been watching you from my office and I've printed out 96 pages of evidence.'

So they completely messed me up, even though all I was doing was blocking stupid porn mail that someone else had subscribed me to. For about a term we weren't allowed to log on as ourselves: we had to use this temporary account.

Some time after this, we got called into the office. He wanted to know the "truth", so we just bluffed it out, saying we were curious and wanted to learn things. Then he said 'Does the word "Rubber Ducky" ring a bell to you?' This was the password of an email account that J___ and I had set up to store programs in. We denied all knowledge of the account, of course, but he gave us a real hard time giving us the evil eyeball. Since then he's always kept an eye on me, so it's hard to get away with anything at all.

Social Engineering & Urban Exploration

Infiltration hacking

I t's unusual for someone to call themselves an infiltration hacker rather than a social-engineering hacker, but it's very much social engineering. In fact, another of my handles, one which I didn't use, was 'The Infiltrator'. I did pick up a lot of social-engineering skills because, unfortunately, I look very young for my age. Universities are 18-plus and there was me, a schoolkid, and I must have been about 14 or 15 at the time. You had to justify why you were there, so you learned to make up stories: anything that would work. 'Oh, I'm here with my brother' or 'I've come to meet my father who's studying part-time', 'I look very young for my age', or even 'I'm thinking about joining the university in a few years' time and I've come in on a open day and was just checking out the computer labs because I want to do computer science.'

Not having a phone line bred me to be a different type of hacker: someone who specialized in infiltrating places, getting on with people and getting their trust and confidence and such like. I went that way because nothing was traceable to me and I could satisfy my curiosity about computers. The other thing in my life was that after my mother died I got into trouble with the police, and got convicted of a crime I didn't commit. It was nothing to do with hacking: it was a charge of interfering with a motor vehicle. I didn't do it, but I was convicted in the courts anyhow. I knew that that the police records database is on computer. My dream is to break into that computer and wipe off that criminal record. I'd love to do it. I've been doing research on it, but it's a very slow process and I haven't got very far. Apparently the best way is to bribe a police officer working on the database to remove the record, but I haven't got the money. Anyhow, that's the criminal route, with all the problems with ethics and morals which that entails.

The other thing which interested me as a teenager was explosives, which I actually learned from *Star Trek*, funnily enough. There's one episode which tells you how to make gunpowder, and that's where it all came from. I never found out what it was called, and I need to know[7]. I knew that on bulletin boards there was all that kind of information which had been banned, and I love any controversial forbidden knowledge. The *Hacker's Handbook* by Hugo Cornwall was allegedly banned, and that's why when he brought out a book about industrial espionage I bought it, in case that got banned too.

There have been different books which have come and gone. *The Anarchist's Cookbook* is another example, and the last time I saw it in Tower Records I didn't have the money to buy it. I like anything controversial, especially where I wasn't meant to have the information, and I'd always try and find out more. Computers were a route into that as well.

---

[7] *Editor's note*: The *Star Trek* episode in question is 'Arena', first shown in 1967, in which aliens transport Captain Kirk to a barren planet to fight an alien Gorn. Kirk wins by synthesizing gunpowder from local ingredients to create a makeshift gun but, importantly, refuses to kill the Gorn even when given the chance to do so.

A lot of the infiltration hacking was just a way into getting access to systems because I wanted to learn more: I was curious. Not having systems at home, losing my ZX81, I wanted to learn about bigger systems, but in those days computers were very expensive. Also, not having a phone line made you specialize in trying to make connections via other phone lines, telephone boxes and suchlike. There was a time when I was involved with someone else, and we beige-boxed from a telephone box, ran off an extension box and connected to the Internet. It wasn't incurring any cost apart from to BT, but I have heard stories where people connected to other people's houses and stuff. This means that they get a big bill, and that isn't fair. A phone box, that's BT, and to me that seems OK ethically and morally compared to connecting to someone's house: it's a large corporation and can afford it.

So I started being an infiltration hacker just by being interested and things and looking for information.

Keys to the kingdom

I keep in touch with what's going on even when I don't hack. I've got all the keys to every single congestion-charging camera in London: the whole lot. I picked them up off the road. They were just sitting there on the pavement: the workmen must have forgotten them when they left. I just took one look and thought, 'Wow', and picked them up. Things like that happen to me. One day I wandered past a large Telco cab box and there was a huge bunch of Telco keys lying on top. I thought they might be useful, so I grabbed them.

These engineers can be really forgetful, they leave stuff lying around and anyone can just pick it up. The other day my local Telco engineer was working away and when he went for lunch in his truck he left his whole bag of tools lying there.

Now, I know this engineer, because I've been socially engineering him for information, so I took his tools home until he finished his lunch and then went back with them. I pointed out that it was lucky it was me who had wandered past and not one of the local thieving scumbags, and he was really grateful. Look after your Telco engineer and he looks after you. This was helpful to me because now he trusts me even more and just gives out all sorts of information. Now I know what all the local cab boxes do. I know the location of the manhole which houses all the police CCTV connections. If someone knocked that out by setting fire to it, all the CCTV cameras in this part of town would be useless. Just down the road from that is another cab box which routes all the burglar alarms for the whole area. Knock that out and all the businesses, banks and ATMs for a block would be vulnerable. It's very easy to find out things like that if you have social-engineering skills. These guys are great: you just walk up and show an interest and they'll chat to you.

People hacking

When you work in IT technical support you get very exasperated with users who can't be bothered to put their brains in gear before calling tech support. A common call is that a monitor or terminal won't come on. You walk down to the user's 'broken' terminal, plug it in and then it springs into life. Of course the user's all apologetic – 'Silly me', and all that. All you can do is reassure them that they aren't stupid, that anyone could have made that mistake, because making the users feel happy is a major part of IT tech support.

It makes you wonder about these people. You know that if their television didn't come on, or their Hoover, or their hairdryer, then the first thing they'd do is check it was plugged in and switched on. Once they're dealing with a computer, their whole mental capacity goes out of the window: they figure it's too complicated for them, and they don't think of checking simple things like power. A lot of people don't realize that managing IT is about managing people as much as managing machines; that the techie side of it is simple compared to the people side.

Sometimes, being a hacker and a social engineer means that you can do things in a different way. At one place I worked, the CEO was given a replacement PA and she had lots of problems with her computer. This meant the CEO was always on my case – the last thing you need when you're looking after another 100 users and servers and a large network. I tried everything with this machine. It was a standard-build PC, identical to all the other PCs which had been built and installed all across the company, with a standard desktop environment and build that we'd tested to destruction. I knew the standard desktop and PC package was bombproof and the fact that no other user reported the same symptoms made me suspicious.

The problems continued, and one day I came up with the solution. I went to the PA and told her I'd swap her machine for my machine. She knew I'd been using the standard build for months and it had been working perfectly, so she agreed immediately. When I took the PC into her office I asked to her to look after my PC, because it had always worked for me. I also told her I wanted her to think of it as her PC now, and to help her 'bond' with it I wanted her to give it a name. She thought I was crazy, but she went along with me and gave it the name Poppy. I pointed out that Poppy was a very good PC, but that sometimes at the end of a long hard day or on a Friday afternoon 'she' could get a little tired. I asked her to 'be nice to Poppy'; I said that if Poppy got tired then she should talk to Poppy nicely and coax her a little and she was more likely to respond.

In the days that followed, I made regular follow-up calls to the PA to see how Poppy was getting along. Surprisingly, the PA now had no problems with the computer at all, and was very happy with Poppy. I never had any problems with that user of that computer again in all the time I was with the company.

That's what I mean by hacking and social engineering helping in an IT techie job. Some techies act all superior to the users and they'd have taken great delight in putting the PA down for her repeated mistakes, but that's an inappropriate way to deal with a user, especially the CEO's PA.

I knew it was human error causing the problem, but instead of blaming her for the errors which had been causing the repeated 'faults', I'd personalized the computer. This allowed the PA to anthromorphize the computer and project those faults as the computer being 'tired'. Once she could do that, she didn't get angry with the computer any more and the very act of coaxing the computer to co-operate made her less likely to commit the error which was causing the problem in the first place. So I actually fixed the computer fault by fixing a bug in the user's wetware, but very subtly, using psychology and social engineering. That's like hacking people, but in a positive way.

Urban exploration

I only heard the phrase 'urban exploration' recently and, when I did, I realized that it is something I've done since my childhood.

One town I lived in had all these old World War Two bunkers and defences. The best thing was that there were a huge number of tunnels underneath these bunkers, linking offices, strongpoints, gun emplacements and ammo stores. We explored these tunnels thoroughly with candles and home-made flaming torches. I think if it had been a few years later we'd have used it for *Dungeons & Dragons*, but that hadn't been invented yet, so we used to play Cowboys and Indians or Hide and Seek. It was the perfect place for both of those games. I remember there was one big old bunker set into the cliff and we could never figure out how to get into it, even though we could see if from outside.

We explored for ages before finding the 'secret' (i.e. well-hidden) tunnel which linked a gun emplacement to this bunker. We used to know which ammo stores had shafts running up to the gun emplacements and we'd call up from below through the long shafts and scare anyone who was above ground, moaning and groaning like the ghosts of forgotten soldiers.

Eventually the authorities decided it was a danger to the children and teenagers who played there. They bricked up the tunnels and cut away a lot of the ladders which allowed access to the roofs of the lookout points. After that, we could get to the tunnels by smashing down the brick and breeze-blocks covering the entrances, but we never had the same level of access again. Years later, they built a modern housing estate on the land. I often wonder if the residents know what's under their feet. If I lived there now, I'd dig down and find the old tunnel system, which would be a useful way of gaining a few hundred square feet of extra space.

Infiltrating groups

I f I want to work my way into any group, I'll always find out what the common interests of the group are. I found out when I was younger that I wanted to learn as much as possible about the world, and I've tried to learn as many different things as possible. This comes in really handy, because I can find common ground with people really quickly.

One time I sat down in a bar next to someone and we were chatting away, and it turned out he was a systems administrator for a large company. I sympathized with his problems, empathized with him and commiserated about how hard his life was as a systems administrator. Once I'd done that, I had him eating out of the palm of my hand and he kept buying me drinks. Now, I've got a high capacity for alcohol, which is good, because I could keep drinking his drinks and talking to him all night long. In the end, he told me loads of things which he shouldn't have. So not only did I get free drinks all night, but I also learned about the computer systems at his company. The point is, he was grateful that I was interested in his job, grateful to have someone to talk to about his work, and once I showed an interest in him my job was done: he did everything else for me.

Infiltration tale

I was hanging around with D___ one weekend – I can't remember when it was – and we were talking about Docklands and Canary Wharf. I'd been up there a few times with H___ war-walking and looking for wireless networks, so I was familiar with the area and knew that there were quite a few interesting networks up there. So D___ had this mad idea about going and checking out this BT building. It was a bank holiday and he wanted to explore this building, and we climbed up the outside steps to the next level. He was trying to climb in through open windows and I was stopping him because I'd noticed that the building wasn't empty. I thought it was a bit hairy. There'd been recent terrorist activity in Canary Wharf and the whole area was on high alert.

We were on this staircase outside the building and these guys came out and wanted to know what we were doing. We bluffed it, saying we were looking for the Docklands Light Railway and were these the right stairs to the station etc. These guys didn't buy our story: they wanted to call the police, and we just said, 'Sure; we're doing nothing wrong, but we're lost.' But when we tried to leave, the police arrived. You can understand why they arrived quickly: Docklands, terrorist alert, BT building – it looked suspicious and it put us in a bit of a spot. Luckily, they questioned me first, and being a social engineer I immediately put on my Spanish accent, explaining that I was lost, and that I was looking for the train station and all that. When they asked me where I lived I made up an address in Barcelona, and told them that I was over here working as a waiter. I'd turned into Manuel from *Fawlty Towers*; but they bought our story and they let us go. It bought us enough time to leave without explaining exactly why we were there. We weren't really doing anything wrong – it was a bit of harmless fun, and the laws of trespass are so vague that it was unlikely that anything would have happened to us.

Exploration

G rowing up as teenager in a small town, drinking, smoking pot and messing around; that was where I was at until I got into computers. We became adept at finding the places where no one would ever go and claiming them for ourselves. We'd climb on to church roofs with a bottle of vodka and a bag of weed and sit there and get trashed. Sometimes we got so trashed that no one could get down again and we'd have to wait until we were sober enough to move. Large trees served the same purpose, and had the same problems. Many a night we'd sit with a bottle of booze purloined from somewhere up a large and accommodating oak tree. On many occasions we'd fall out of the tree in giggling heaps as we slipped over each other like drunken eels when imaginary handholds vanished in the dark. How we never broke any bones at that time always amazes me.

Churchyards and ruined buildings were, and still are, favourite places. No one goes to a churchyard or abandoned building, especially after dark. That's because they're scared of being mugged, scared of the dark, scared of everything. In those days, we were fearless. We knew damned well that nobody and nothing was going to stop us from what we wanted to do. We'd go anywhere, climb anything and explore any space.

We knew that at the top of the stairs at a multi-storey car park there was a ledge and that no one ever went there because they all left their cars on the lower decks so they kept cool. We used to have parties up on that ledge. We knew that the local ruins in the centre of town were climbable, that you could scale the broken walls and climb to another level where there was enough space for a dozen people to sit. We used to have parties up there. We knew where the underground tunnels of the local mall were, how to access the service spaces in the local university. None of us was doing a degree, but the whole university was a big playground with towers and tunnels, secret passageways and unexpected exits.

Even now I like to find hidden, forbidden or secret places to explore. There's a group of us who like nothing more than to have a party in some strange place. We take food, disposable barbeques, booze and a beatbox and we go and party there. When we leave we take everything with us – all the rubbish, everything – so that no one knows we were even there. When I go on holiday, I prefer exploring ruins to anything else. I get bored with a beach holiday, but give me some ruins and I'm quite content. I think it goes back to those early days when I loved exploration for its own sake.

A Hacker's Life

Novice hacker

I'm older than the average hacker, so I grew up in the age of the Apollo moon shots, the Beatles, Woodstock and the Vietnam War.

I was mad about science fiction, mad about space travel, mad about music. But I was born just a little too early for the personal computer boom. I had a chemistry set instead: not a dinky little boxed thing like everyone else had, but a large semi-professional chemistry set which would put many school labs to shame these days.

Why was it so big? Well, it wasn't because I was a rich kid who could afford to spend loads of money on chemistry equipment. It was because I used to track down and buy chemistry equipment from proper chemistry suppliers; half-litres of nitric acid, pipettes, beakers, dishes and retorts. I'd save my money, then send in an order with payment, and I'd *never* mention that I was only 13 years old. But they never checked my age. The order was paid for, the handwriting looked adult and they always shipped the stuff.

The other reason my chemistry set was so good is that anything I didn't have I'd make. I became an expert at recycling batteries for zinc and carbon, or using lye and aluminium to make hydrogen, then using the hydrogen to make weak hydrochloric acid. I'd do anything to get hold of ingredients easily and cheaply, and I used to make a lot of my own apparatus, even doing some glassblowing.

I now realize that this was the hacker in me trying to get out. The reason why my chemistry set was bigger and better than anyone was because it was a *hacker's* chemistry set. It's just that the hacker didn't know what hacking was, had never heard of hackers, because personal computers were still a number of years in the future. Computers were remote objects kept in large, white, air-conditioned rooms, where only the faithful could worship at the high altar of information technology. At the age of 13, my idea of a cool computer was Hal 9000 from *2001*, even though it went totally bananas by the end of the film.

I was a typical proto-hacker; underachieving at school, and my reports always said, 'Could do better if he tried'. I had retreated beyond school into a world of thought – 'a rich internal life', as the child psychologists used to say. I was obsessed with everything I found interesting, to the exclusion of everything else. I was the archetypal nerd before I ever heard the term. At the age of 13 I could recite every NASA space mission to date and, when they were manned, give the names of the crews.

I finally wrote my first computer program at the age of 16. That sounds quite late now, but in the Seventies that was early. I remember that I'd dropped out of school but used to turn up so see old friends, and one one occasion they said, 'We're going to a one-day computer course at E___ University to learn about computers. Why don't you come along?'

Apparently there was a big drive to attract more promising students to Computer Science degrees, and it worked by giving 16-year-olds the hands-on experience of writing computer programs. Of course, I had no intention of learning computers. After all, the computer bods were good at mathematics, and I was crap at mathematics, so what was the point in learning about computers? But it sounded like a laugh, so I tagged along.

My first program didn't do anything very interesting. The program printed out the lyrics for "Ten Green Bottles" and the initial number of bottles was hard-coded. It was written in ALGOL-60 on punch cards at a punch card terminal, given to white-coated operators who then loaded the cards into a hopper and ran the program for you while you waited to pick up the printout at the other side – the user side – of the computing room.

I remember that they encouraged you to solve problems and add on bells and whistles to make the program better; nice formatting, and an IF clause to see when you no longer needed the 's' on 'bottles' because it was the last bottle.

After the course finished, I was all fired up. I didn't want to stop programming computers, but it was a prerequisite to have mathematics in those days. I drifted off into other things. Eventually, I forgot all about this programming course, and with hindsight it only became relevant again when I became a hacker – or maybe when I started to identify myself as a hacker.

The real deal had to wait another six years or so before I became interested in computers again.

At that time I used to spend a lot of time playing games; role-playing games (*Dungeons & Dragons*, *Traveller*, Steve Jackson games (*Raid on Iran*, *CarWars*, *Dracula*), SimPubs/SPI simulation battle games (*NATO*, *Sniper*, *World War II*), miniature war games, (why were the old geezers so obsessive about the accuracy of the uniforms?) and any other game I could get my hands on, from Monopoly to backgammon. This would later prove to be important on my journey to becoming a hacker.

I'd long forgotten about all computer programming stuff when I finally met K___ some time around 1982 or 1983.

For a long time friends had been telling me that that 'K____ is a computer hacker who lived for computers' and that 'I had to meet K___' because 'we had so much in common' and that we were bound to 'hit it off together' because we were 'so alike'.

When I finally met him, I found K___ was a year or so older than myself, had actually gone to E___ University and had studied computers. When I met him he lived in a ramshackle house surrounded by old industrial control systems, RS232 terminals, skip-recycled Z80 single-board computers and a nice, shiny, new Dragon 32 computer.

Did we hit it off? Did we have a lot in common? Oh, yes! If it weren't for K___, I wouldn't be here now telling you this story.

K___ got me started on this whole computer thing.

K___ encouraged me to learn about computers.

Without K___, I would never have become a hacker.

It started like this:

K___ and I would have conversations and eventually we would start talking about computers. I would show a vague interest and the conversation would get deeper, and then K___ would try and encourage me to buy a computer.

I always responded the same way – 'What do I need a box with buttons on for?' – and he'd laugh, and the conversation would turn to something else.

One weekend it happened that K___ was going away to see his parents and asked if I wanted to borrow his Dragon 32 for the weekend. He said: 'It's got lots of games. It's easy to use and I'll drop it round Saturday.'

When it arrived with all the leads, cassette tapes, a little cassette recorder for loading games and a big pile of manuals, I was somewhat daunted. He showed me how to switch it on, how to load the games, how to use the manuals, and then left me to it.

It took about 24 hours of playing the crappy little 8-bit games before I got bored with the whole thing. I couldn't see the point. The games were so sub-Pong that they didn't hold my interest. The only one which was interesting was a little adventure game based on the original *Colossal Cave* program by Willie Crowther and Don Woods, but that only held my interest because it was so similar to the role-playing games I was familiar with: *Dungeons & Dragons* and *Traveller*.

During all the time I played with this computer I'd been using the manuals to look things up, but it wasn't until I got bored with the games that I found the BASIC manual and started to play around with the BASIC interpreter inside the machine.

The examples weren't very good, but it was fun entering them and playing around with them for a while, when suddenly in the middle of the session I remembered programming the lyrics for "Ten Green Bottles" when I was 16.

With what I'd learnt that day, just remembering the program had once existed was enough to get me started on writing the "Ten Green Bottles" program again. This time I wrote it in Dragon32 BASIC.

I used what I'd learnt from the examples to write a new program, run it, debug it and make it work.

It was a very important moment for me.

That was the day a computer stopped being a box with buttons on.

That was the day that I got hooked on computers.

That was the day that I started to become a hacker.

After this I wanted a computer badly, and eventually I was lucky enough to get my hands on a BBC Model B.

The Acorn-manufactured BBC B looks primitive now, but at the time, against its competitors, it represented the state of the art in home computers. It had a decent BASIC interpreter with built-in 6502 assembler, A/D converters, I/O buses and expansion ports. This, coupled with a properly documented operating system with proper system calls, made this machine a hacker's delight back in 1983.

One of the reasons I wanted a computer was because of the games. Like I said, I played a lot of games, and many of these games involved a lot of repetitive dice-throwing and calculation. It immediately struck me that a properly programmed computer could take a lot of the donkey work out of running moderated games. Soon after that, I became more familiar with text-based adventure games and began to write one of these.

It then became apparent that the limited memory of the BBC wouldn't hold much text for descriptions, especially if entered into the system as BASIC arrays, which was the easiest and logical way to do it for a novice. What was needed was a neater, more compact way of holding descriptions, which didn't have the overhead of storing BASIC arrays and left more memory clear.

I'd heard about machine code and assembler and understood that it was more efficient and compact to write, especially on a machine with only 32K of memory. I knew that all the *real* applications were written in assembly language. I went out and bought a book on programming the BBC assembler and a book about 6502 assembly language. Then I set to work.

The initial solution involved storing the descriptions as continuous text strings in the memory and keeping a table of lengths of the strings. This was indexed such that when you looked up string (x) you looked up the length of string (x) and its address in memory, then called a small routine to call the system call to print out the characters one by one.

Eventually I realized that this was an inelegant solution, and that the extra code needed to maintain the string length table was redundant because I could place a marker byte at the end of each description string which would flag the routine to stop printing the string. For my marker byte I chose 0x0D, because I could print it and it would force a carriage return and still terminate my routine. I had no concept of the C language at this time and the idea of a 0x00 to terminate my strings, otherwise I would have chosen that instead.

Because of the limited memory of the BBC, I was soon deeply immersed in the whole compaction process to get more out of less. The next thing I figured out was that many of the descriptions used the same words over and over again. I knew I would save even more memory by placing a table of the words used in the descriptions and giving each word a unique address, then coding each description as a list of bytes that made the list of words. Instead of having to store all the common words such as 'the', 'and', 'go', 'west', 'up', 'down' in every description, I could now store a single byte for each common word in every description, saving tons more precious memory space.

While I was in the middle of all this 6502 assembly language coding, K___ obtained a set of stepper motors, then designed and built a BBC interface using Darlington transistors. The only thing we had to do now was program the BBC to get the motors to do what we wanted.

We started simply enough with a routine which would turn the motor a prescribed number of steps in any direction, but we became more ambitious. We wanted to run our stepper motors as a program in the background while doing other things, and for that we had to master the black art of interrupt-driven programming. What this meant is that we could set hardware timers in the computer which would automatically run our program when we wanted, but in the background rather than as a main task.

We started by using the BBC hardware to provide the interrupts, but soon realized that we didn't have enough. We started looking at the BBC operating system itself.

Remember I said the BBC was a hacker's delight with a real OS and properly documented system calls? This made it really easy to hook our routine into one of the system interrupts so that every time the computer used that system call, it would run our code for us. This also meant that we didn't have to program the hardware timers because the computer and the operating system did all the work for us. All you had to do was grab the current state of the machine, store it somewhere, run your extra code and then restore the current state of the machine and it went on its way, none the wiser.

I later found out that there was a word to describe software like this. It's called 're-entrant'. It would have helped to have known this beforehand.

Somehow my love of war gaming and my desire to master computers had led me into the darkest crevices of machine code programming. In just over a year I had gone from coding *Ten Green Bottles* to writing interrupt-driven stepper motor drivers and worrying about whether the code was re-entrant or not.

Suddenly the computer had become more important than anything else. I had learnt to love playing with the technology for the fun of playing with it.

I had become a novice hacker.

Exploration

The next step in my evolution as a hacker happened almost by accident when I was accepted at E___ University to study cog-nitive psychology at degree level. Once I got there, I set about trying to take as many computer-related courses as possible.

The first hurdle was my lack of formal training in mathematics. I was supposed to do a first-year course in sociology but preferred the idea of a PASCAL programming course instead. After much fast talking I was finally interviewed by a crusty professor of computer science who looked at me over his glasses and declared that if could I could pass the numerical analysis module, then he would take me on. He offered the course notes for the previous year's module, and when I took one look at this handout my heart sank. It was nothing but equations and weird squiggles which I later found out meant something called 'integration'. Giving no sign that I was worried, I declared that I would be able to do this. 'Sign me up,' I said, and so I started my first formal programming course.

I don't remember much about the course other than that we used UCSD P-System PASCAL on these huge slow Z80 boxes. The P-system PASCAL compiled code into runable modules in an imaginary P-Code, which was then run under a p-system virtual machine.

When they finally taught me about recursion, the first program I wrote was a recursive version of the *Ten Green Bottles* program. More than nine years after I had written my first program in ALGOL-60, I was back at E___ University learning programming for real.

When it came to the numerical analysis module I was really nervous, but they had changed the contents of the course to make it less formal. I ended up writing a PASCAL program to integrate the area under a curve using Romberg's Rule, and eventually passed the course.

Sometime around this point K____ found a whole load of 6809 microcomputers in a skip, along with the antique dumb terminals used to connect to them. These boxes were designed for teaching physics students how to program industrial control systems. They ran an operating system called FLEX, came with a very primitive editor, some utilities, an assembler and linker and a PASCAL compiler. We saw this as a perfect machine to drive the stepper motors, because it would take the load off the BBC's CPU, yet could communicate with the BBC at the same time using the serial port.

To make this machine do anything useful we had to start from scratch and write our own utilities, but the editor was so gruesome that writing and debugging code was a nightmare. We figured there had to be a better way to do things. The BBC had an excellent text editor, so couldn't we use the BBC to write code and then port it to the FLEX system? This would mean that the only time we would have to use the FLEX editor was to fix bugs and simple mistakes, as the bulk of the code could be typed in using the BBC.

The solution was technical, inelegant and clunky, but it worked, so it must count as some kind of hack. We used a cut-down, two-wire serial lead but looped the RTS/CTS on the BBC so that there was no hardware handshaking. We then opened the editor on the FLEX system, put it into insert mode, hooked up the BBC and *spooled* the text straight into the FLEX text editor. When it had finished we unplugged the serial cable, plugged the terminal back in, took the editor out of insert mode and saved the file. After a bit of tidying, we could then compile and run it using the PASCAL compiler which came with the FLEX box.

At university I soon made the welcome discovery that

cognitive psychology was heavily related to artificial intelligence, and this made it easier to gain access to more computers. I signed up for a LISP course, which gave access to the TOPS-20 mainframe, and a PROLOG course, which gave me access to a GEC Unix box, so I could begin to learn Unix.

I wrote semantic memory systems and miniature expert systems. After reading *Neuromancer* by William Gibson I became fascinated by AI and soon became heavily involved in researching symbolic AI approaches to language understanding and narrative comprehension. Using the AI models as a guide, I would design and run psychological experiments using adult and child subjects. It wasn't pioneering work, but it met with a degree of success.

At the end of my degree I was offered a PhD place at B___ University to study experimental psychology. They wanted to use a more computational approach to the study of narrative comprehension, and thought that the work done at E___ had been promising.

When I arrived, the first thing I did was to gain as much access to as many computers as possible. This was easy: as a PhD student you got many more privileges than undergraduates, including external email for the first time. I managed to get a shared office opposite the computer room so I could 'pick up my printouts easily', and became familiar with the PDP-11 and the VAX-11/780, learning the C language and VMS. I started to explore the Joint Academic Network (JANET), an early pre-Internet network using X25, which was only open to UK universities and research institutes, and I also explored the campus-wide VAX cluster.

I was working late every night in the office, having a great time playing with the university computer systems, but what I wasn't doing was any PhD work. When the crunch came at the end of the academic year, I left B___ University behind.

All the time I was at those universities, I was learning and exploring computers, but I had never accessed computer systems which I was not authorized to use. I was a computer enthusiast, but I wasn't a hacker. I hadn't crossed over yet: that was still a year in the future.

When I left B___ University, I was fortunate enough to be offered a position as a research assistant at my old university. I was back in a soft science department with few computers and a heavy workload, so my proto-hacking activities were curtailed for some time. I was heavily involved in running psychological experiments, testing AI models against human data, using statistics packages such as SPSS to analyze the results and then writing the conclusions into reports. I didn't have time to play with computers as much as I would have liked, but the work was intellectually challenging and sufficiently computer-based to satisfy all my technology needs.

It was only when the entire research team moved universities to set up shop in the middle of a computer science department that I started to get really busy. I was lucky enough to be in a computer science department when things were really interesting, and getting more so. Our systems administrator was as keen as mustard, so he was always installing new software for us to play with and upgrading old software to make it better.

We had all the latest GNU software, which was patched and upgraded as soon as it was available: we had PERL before anyone had heard of the World Wide Web: and, more importantly, we had access to USENET.

Suddenly I was plunged into a whole new world of learning.

The computer science department was still part of the JANET network, but because it was more computer-focused we had more toys, and thus far more access to computers, earlier than many of the hackers I know today. This must have been 1989 or so, and the JANET network was still fully X25. In those days, if you wanted to hop on to the 'Internet', the US research network, you needed to learn how to get there.

At the time, there were several experimental JANET–Internet gateways, many of them allowing anonymous access to the academic community. Once you knew where there was, say, a telnet gateway or ftp gateway, then you could access that computer, and through it you could access the Internet.

About this time I bought an Amiga. I'd been playing with the Sun workstations at the university, enhancing my Unix knowledge, and decided I wanted a multi-tasking machine with a Unix-like operating system. The department was using MINIX, but the cost of PC hardware put me off, so I plumped for the Amiga instead. Once I had the computer, I knew that I wanted GNU tools for the machine, but wasn't sure how to get them on to the Amiga. I was familiar with the file transfer program Kermit, which I used all the time between micro-computers and larger mainframes or servers, and understood that a Kermit implementation was available for the Amiga. I located it on a Fred Fish disk, stuck it on to a 100K BBC micro floppy disk and took it home.

Of course, once I got the program home, I still had one minor problem: how to get this program on to the Amiga. I thought about it for a while and then dug out the serial cable I'd used to transfer files from the BBC to the FLEX box and hooked the two machines together. Then I sat down and wrote two programs; the first, in BBC BASIC, opened a file and stuffed the file byte-by-byte down the serial port, the second, in Amiga BASIC, opened a file and then stuffed bytes from the serial port into that file. It was kludgy as hell, didn't use any hardware or software handshaking and ran slowly, but it allowed me to transfer Kermit to the Amiga and boot-strap myself to another level. Now I had Kermit running on both BBC and Amiga it was easy to download software from the Internet, put it on a BBC disk, take it home, transfer it to the Amiga and run it.

Nowadays we take the Internet and Open Source for granted, but back in those days this was a big deal. Other computer-literate friends without access to the Internet began asking for software and for a while I became like a physical real world-to-Internet gateway, putting anything from 3D models to Open Source software on to disks and mailing it to friends all around the UK.

So it began. I would hang around on USENET, could find my way around ftp sites, logged on to MUDS and generally started poking around the Internet.

About this time a friend at college complained about not being able to use his email account to contact friends. This was because his email account was an undergraduate account and thus restricted to internal mail only.

Because I was familiar with the Sun systems he was using, I knew that those particular systems allowed you to set up a file, called a '.forward' file, to redirect mail if you were away from the campus for any time. I showed him how to write the email address of the person he wanted to contact into the .forward file, send email to himself and then delete the .forward file afterwards. This had the effect of directing mail to whoever he wanted on the Internet, regardless of the restrictions placed on him by his college.

It was a very small hack, but it helped him a lot.

In the end, it was more than a year of learning about the Internet, coupled with reading things on USENET, which precipitated me into crossing the line between computer enthusiast hacker and system security hacker.

Crossing the line

I was reading *Computer Underground Digest* (CUD) on USENET one day and decided that I wanted to read more, so I headed off for the CUD archives. While I was there, I noticed a whole bunch of other stuff with names like LOD and PHRACK and I grabbed a load of that too.

Eventually I got round to reading some of it and it was a revelation to me. I printed out the entire collection of LOD files on the fast departmental printer, took it home and sat up long into the night reading what I'd found. When I fell asleep that night, my head was buzzing with ideas. The discovery of the computing underground was a revelation to me, and although some of the techniques described in LOD seemed more relevant to the USA than England, I was determined to try some of them out.

The first thing I did was write my own Trojan in the C language. This was the most unsubtle Trojan you could imagine: it emulated the login sequence of the local Unix server through a PAD which then connected to a vt100 terminal. You logged in as yourself, left the program running, and when someone tried to log in it logged the userid and password before giving a 'down for maintenance' or 'password incorrect' message.

Later on I wrote a fuller version which emulated a campus-wide PAD and allowed you to select any computer on campus which anyone would normally log in to, then emulated the banners and login prompts for any of those computers – about 30 or so across campus. As you can imagine, this gathered a lot of userids and passwords but never, to my chagrin, the root password. It turned out that our systems admininstrator was way too canny, and only ever logged on as root from his personal console in his office.

My next exploration of system security hacking was a little more interesting. The campus was covered with serial concentrators, which interfaced all the serial terminals to the Ethernet system.

At this time Ethernet, even 10-base-2 'cheapernet', was an expensive proposition reserved for research workstations such as Sun 3s and the occasional PC or Mac. Because of this, most access to JANET and thus to the Internet was via these serial ports. For example, to transfer files from the Internet I'd fire up a vt100 terminal, log into an Ethernet computer such as a Sun and then use Unix commands to connect to the Internet gateways. Once I'd transferred my files from the Internet to the gateway I could then use JANET to transfer the file to my local server, and from there I'd use a copy of Kermit to transfer the file to a BBC floppy disk.

Because of the huge number of BBC microcomputers attached to serial ports connected to JANET, there were a large number of interesting things to do with these spare BBC microcomputers.

I started by capturing the list of all academic addresses at the NISS database, then massaged them into a manageable format using standard Unix tools. I now had a list of all JANET-connected computers along with their operating system type and their JANET addresses. Using this data, I constructed a BBC BASIC program which attempted to connect to every computer on this using the default and common passwords I'd found in the LOD files. I used to set this program up on a Friday night and come back after the weekend to see how many JANET computers I'd found valid logins for. There used to be a lot.

In those days, there wasn't the interest in computer security that there is now. To begin with, many Unix systems were shipped with default passwords. Then there was the fact that within academia, many users were given easy default passwords. Finally, users themselves chose stupid passwords. It wasn't too hard to get hold of valid logins and passwords across the JANET system.

It seems basic and crude now, and that's because it was. It wasn't for another couple of years that I began to see proper TCP/IP hacks and buffer overflows, so a lot of the attention of hackers was focused on passwords and social engineering.

My next hacking escapade didn't go quite so well. Using the example code by Shooting Shark in the LOD files, I began to write a Unix password cracker. Because the local systems administrator was clever enough to figure out what the C code was for, I chose to write it on a system belonging to another department in the university. I wanted to use a Sun, because I was familiar with Suns, so I signed on for a beginner's course at the physics department across campus, pretending to be ignorant of computers. I was quickly bagged.

The staff at the tutorial session realized that I knew a damn sight more Unix than they did and reported this to the system manager, who checked what was in my directory and reported me to the systems administrator, who cut off my access and phoned me up demanding an interview.

At the interview I was brazen, claiming I was a computer enthusiast interested in security. I said the only reason that I had written the damn program was due to 'academic curiosity'. The systems administrator *hated* me. He knew damn well that there was more to it, but I was a staff member with a professor who brought in lots of funding and prestige, and in the end academic politics counts for more than anything.

Luckily for me, the university authorities didn't seem to take the whole thing too seriously; my boss was annoyed, my departmental head was annoyed and the local systems administrator was annoyed, but the Vice-Chancellor of the university who disciplined me had a twinkle in his eye. I think in a university environment it was expected that intelligent people would get up to mischief, and compared with a lot of other drunken university pranks my transgression was mild in the extreme.

However, the upshot of all this was that I stopped hacking. Everyone was on my case – my professor, my boss, my departmental head – and to cap it all, the systems administrator and I were no longer on speaking terms. I thought it a premature end to what had looked like a promising career as a hacker, but I was wrong: fate had another twist in store for me.

Later that year the research grant I had been working on finished, and it was time to move on. Somehow I managed to land a job at L___ University working in a lab funded by the MRC. This was a whole new kettle of fish for me. In one fell swoop I'd gone from being surrounded by computer science students to being surrounded by psychologists engaged in medical research. They still had computers, of course, but the focus wasn't on computers, and with my computing skills I soon became the laboratory systems administrator.

I now had total control over an entire network of computers attached to the Internet and could begin to explore things a lot more thoroughly. It also had the ultimate effect of drawing me deeper into the hacker scene, where I would learn to share information with other hackers and to work with them to achieve certain goals.

It started simply enough when I decided to run a warez site using fsp, a connectionless UDP-based protocol much favoured by warez traders at the time, on the hard disk of the Unix computer assigned to me for my research. I then got an anonymous email address at the late, lamented anon@penet.fi.

This meant I could trade warez with like-minded people, collecting software on my server. At the same time, I began using IRC and it soon became commonplace for me to remain logged into IRC all day with a window in the top right-hand corner of my screen, one eye on the conversations as I worked at my day job.

As the warez site became more popular it became better known, and eventually some 'anti-warez' dude announced my server's IP address to an entire newsgroup for all the world to see. By then, the hard drive in my server was chittering constantly like a restless hamster as people from all over the world accessed the vast array of resources on offer. There were more than 800Mb of warez[8] at the point I pulled the plug, which was about 30 seconds after I read my IP address on USENET.

By then, I had established myself. Other cyber denizens knew me and we were sharing information on a regular basis. I regularly spoke on IRC to hackers all around the world, but the first time I went to a hacker gathering was a unique revelation about the potential of hacker culture.

I'd heard about *2600* magazine a number of years ago and had never seen a copy, but through a fortuitous set of circumstances I managed to get hold of one. On finding out about *2600* meetings, I immediately asked the other hackers on IRC if there were any in the UK. It turned out someone had heard there was a meeting in London but had never attended because they were from Manchester or somewhere. Eventually I tracked down someone who knew where the London meeting was and went to my first one.

I was amazed at the number of people who turned up at

[8] *Editor's note*: It doesn't seem a lot now, but at that time the average PC memory size was 4–16Mb and the average PC hard disk 20–40Mb.

the meetings, talking about computers, fiddling with devices, swapping information and having a great time. Very soon I became a *2600* regular, meeting many UK hackers for whom I have a lot of respect even now. Someone said to me recently that those were the 'great days' of London 2600, but I'm not sure if I agree: it just seemed great because it was all new and the Internet was just starting to take off in a big way.

I remember that to get my first home Internet connection I used a hacked account on a university dialup system to log in to a Unix box connected to the Internet. I'd log in with this really slow 2400-baud modem and then use the bandwidth of JANET to connect to IRC, send email or transfer files. Then I would use Kermit to fetch the files down from the compromised server to my home PC. I used this system to connect to the Internet from home right up until the time Demon started their consumer service, then bought a 9600-baud modem and signed up with them.

Meanwhile, back at work I'd become seriously involved with a group of hackers who hung out on IRC. It had started to get even more fun because I'd finally learned about ICMP nuking. None of us thought anything of knocking down an IRC server somewhere in the world just so we could get the channel operator's status on a channel. These days it's called denial of service, but we were just having fun: we were heavily involved in what used to be called 'IRC Wars', and at the time that was almost more important to us than the real world.

We would break into computers to install IRC relays to cover our tracks while playing with IRC. These were like proxy servers which ran on a compromised server listening to some port and then connected you to an IRC server. The IRC server would log you as coming from the IP of the compromised machine. Later on, the technique was extended when someone gave me the code for a telnet relay. That way

I could log into a computer anywhere in the world and it would show up as the compromised machine. It was great for covering your tracks, because you could go through more than one of them.

To actually gain access to these computers, I used a variety of techniques. I liked using YPX because it was a nice, easy, remote hack which gave you a whole password file for very large networks. Sometimes you'd get a password file with 10,000 users on it.

I used to use Alex Muffet's Crack to process these files and had a dictionary with more than 1.5 million words culled from USENET and various online dictionaries in many languages. I made a point of seeking out and getting copies of dictionaries, which wasn't hard given that I was working in AI research. With a fast Unix workstation, a copy of Crack and a large dictionary I never had any problems finding logins for NIS-based systems all over the world.

Eventually it all came to an end. The University figured out that all this bandwidth was being chewed up from my subnet and investigated while I was away. When I returned to work, I was locked out of the system. Yet again I was in a position where I had to defend my somewhat unconventional use of university computer systems. I played the standard 'intellectual curiosity' card, but this time my employers weren't having any of it. In the end we compromised, so I ended up quitting academia and getting a better-paid job in commercial IT instead. Of course, I didn't stop hacking, but it was the beginning of the end for me.

I remained a *2600* regular for a number of years, attended the first 'Access All Areas' and kept current on a number of BBSs devoted to hacking. I had my home network and continued to try out different things; it's just that I took a much lower profile on the hacker scene.

Later on, when a couple of hackers with whom I'd been involved in setting up IRC relays got busted, I decided I'd finally had enough and quit the scene altogether.

I deleted the files on my hard drive, got rid of the hacker tools and chucked out my passwords and userids. I dropped a whole pile of BT documents, manuals, clothing and tools, along with my beige box, into a skip.

The only thing I kept was my beloved *2600* BlueBox T-shirt, which was to lead me into another adventure entirely – but that's another story.

At this point I was finished; I'd stopped being a hacker. I stopped going to *2600* meetings, I stopped using IRC, I stopped reading *PHRACK* and *2600* magazines and I hardly even bothered to use the Internet. I had dropped out of the hacking scene. For me, it was all over. I had become an ex-hacker.

Phreaking & Wi-Fi

University PBX

I knew a phreaker when I was at university who we'll call MacBeth (not his real handle). In our second year, a company came to the university and installed telephones in all the halls of residence. The computer nerds amongst us greeted this with much joy, because now we would be able to tie into the campus network without having to leave our campus flats – which is where, in fact, many of us spent the next three years!

Desperate to explore the new possibilities offered by access to the internal phone network, MacBeth fired up his copy of Toneloc and went to work. I think it took him about two weeks of running Toneloc overnight to map out the whole network. He found various modems, and received several phone calls from people he'd managed to page in the middle of the night.

But what MacBeth *really* wanted was a way out of the campus network. Could he find out how to defeat the charging scheme on the telephone system? Partly this was because he was just that kind of person, but the deal with the phones was that you had to register with the Telco, get an ID and PIN and suchlike. They were only on the campus for the first two weeks, and were notoriously hard to get hold of after that. During those two weeks, MacBeth was never sober enough, or up early enough, to deal sensibly with queuing up and filling in forms and registering, so MacBeth didn't have his own ID and PIN, and in fact couldn't make any external phone calls at all.

I got the sense that he was also rather upset by the monopoly the Telco held over the students, and the fact that they wouldn't carry 0800 calls over their network. That meant several things he was used to being able to access wouldn't be available to him, and the thought of a telephone which limited his activity in any way was not pleasing.

He had found the computer which controlled the PBX to which all the phones were connected, but it was a dialback system, and using a different line to dial out on, so it couldn't be tricked by any method he knew of.

MacBeth was running out of ideas. He was burned out by late nights sitting watching each number on the 100,000-line exchange being dialled, listening to the responses and making notes, and gutted that he still couldn't get calls off the campus.

He wondered if there might be some other way to achieve his goal, and began tapping almost at random (apparently) at the phone keypad. Less than 30 minutes later, he'd done it. Just like that. There was a way to fool the system into thinking it had received a valid logon for external calls when in fact it hadn't.

I was stunned. Two weeks of exploration had yielded much data, but no leads on his ultimate goal, so he sat down with the handset and just cracked it. I've never seen anything like it, before or since, and I'm pretty sure he hadn't either. He was elated.

MacBeth took advantage of this to call BBSs both in the UK and abroad, on both normal and premium-rate numbers. He did this for about three months, and then he decided it was time to stop. He came to this decision, I think, because he knew (or thought he knew) that sooner or later someone was going to figure out what was going on, and he was going to get busted.

He 'ummed' and 'ahhhd' about this for quite some time, and eventually he came up with a solution. He would tell some people he had heard of a method to get free calls. They, naturally, would use it, and they would tell other people, he was sure. This would have three effects. Firstly, it would cover his ass; it would be funny to think of all those students getting free calls; and, of course, MacBeth could keep using the method until the hole was closed, as he would just be one of many.

It worked far better than he could ever have imagined.

For another three months, the campus buzzed, as the method went around and around and met itself coming back. MacBeth even had people tell him about it in pubs, claiming to know the guy who had discovered it.

It went on for so long, and became so widely known, that faculty staff were using it to make personal calls which weren't logged on their departments' itemized bills (for which they were required to pay).

MacBeth began to worry: his plan had been that the increased activity would alert the Telco to the hole, and they would close it without bothering to check the background too carefully, thus leaving him safe and free. But this was getting silly; people were spending up to eight hours on the phone to Greece, China and Africa. The Telco was, in fact, 'losing' more revenue than it could ever possibly have made from legitimate call traffic.

Eventually, in the fourth month, the hole closed. For three days MacBeth chewed his nails, and considered what he would do if he were held responsible for the total of calls made.

Even the most conservative estimate suggested that the 'cost' in lost revenue would run into millions of pounds, and MacBeth knew that some people had been dialling into things like premium-rate chat lines and sex lines for hours and hours at a time every day for the last four months.

He began to suspect that he was going to do prison time, possibly for a very long time. But then something very strange indeed happened.

News reached him that someone had been arrested for stealing phone calls. Naturally, he was beyond himself at this point.

As it later transpired, what had happened was that a girl in one of the halls who was (or had become) a devout Christian had turned up at her hall tutor's door in tears and confessed to her that she had committed a sin by stealing free phone calls. Being of a sensitive nature, the hall tutor immediately called the police and campus security. The girl was arrested and was held overnight. She was questioned for around eight hours (or so we heard) by the police, members of the Telco's security department and university staff. She was released without charge.

There were desultory attempts to investigate: the police and Telco weenies questioned everyone else in the girl's hall; but then they stopped. We can only guess at why. No one was ever charged.

Less than a year later, the university contracted a different Telco to run its campus phones.

Cellular

I didn't really get into phreaking, but I got into cellular. I had an NEC P3 which was chipped and just needed the codes to make it work. The old analogue mobile phones needed two numbers: the Electronic Serial Number (ESN) and the MIN, which was the telephone number, and you needed to have both those numbers programmed into the phone to make free calls. Now, I had the modified phone with the modchip, which had a hacked EPROM, but I didn't have a scanner to pick up the ESN/MIN pairs out of the airwaves. They're just unencrypted radio waves, so it's really easy to scan the right frequencies and get the numbers.

The problem was that I didn't have the technology or equipment to do the scanning, so I couldn't get hold of the numbers I needed. I didn't figure it was right, because I could-n't get my own numbers, and being reliant on someone else is something that I've always hated. I always like to cut out the middleman. Later on I went to a boot fair and picked up an old RAC car kit phone, like a Motorola brick phone: you can modify them to act as a scanner, but by then the technology was getting obsolete as they phased out analogue phones.

You could also trade the ESN/MIN pairs from bulletin boards and other places, so it was very easy to get free calls from cellular phones, but I was uneasy about the ethics of the whole thing, especially when you were relying on other people to supply you with the ESN/MIN pairs. I think the early 1990s, when they made chipping phones illegal, was about the time I stopped. Once it was no longer a grey area, I wasn't interested.

Cybercafe

I was never into BBSs much because I didn't have a phone line. The one BBS that I really got into was CyberCafe, Heath Bunting's BBS site. I used to get information from there, and occasionally went up to Cyberia to their meetings, where I would meet all sorts of strange people. There was this weird guy who was into alien abductions, an older chap, and he was just obsessed by it: he was trying to set up an 'alien embassy'. The CyberCafe BBS was really very good; I ran up a few friends' phone bills calling that. BBSs died when the Internet came along, but I believe they'll come back. The Internet isn't private enough: it's too well monitored. Anyone can run a BBS at home, and access is more private. Old-school communications using computers with private BBSs allow much more private communication. I think the hacker scene benefited from things like that: it was less visible.

People would learn how to scan exchanges for hosts and then find these BBSs and think, 'Wow! There are other people like me out there.' All that scanning is interesting. The Americans were way ahead on technology, and they bene-fited from low-cost or free phone calls within the same area code, but in the UK we were more restricted: we had to scan 0800 freephone numbers. Nowadays BT look for things like scans on 0800 numbers, but you used to be able to do it, and there were a lot of scans of 0800 numbers circulating on BBSs. It'd cost me a fortune to scan my own area code from my own phone, so I don't do it. That's why we do hand scans of 0800 numbers from phones rather than from home, or use a mobile phone.

Some mobile phone tariffs allow free local calls after 7pm, so if you co-ordinated several people you could scan a very large area of the city for free. It's not financially viable to scan large areas from your own phone, so what's needed is some-where from which you can scan large numbers of comput-ers, and that means a large number of modems. That kind of thing really interests me: if you had access to a computer with 40 modems and 40 phone lines, you could scan whole area exchanges really quickly. With 40 modems at your disposal and an average of one minute per call, you could

scan an entire area code in around four hours. But you would-
n't scan an entire area code over four hours; you'd interleave
the calls with other area codes to hide the wardialler so you
didn't get detected.

This seems like fiction, but there are people out there
running online operations with that many modems at their
disposal, so it's not hard to find one of these computers and
'own it'. Once you do, you interleave the calls you make with
the calls which normally go out of that block of modems, so
the scan gets lost in the multiple calls which would normally
get made. If you just took over the machine, owned it and
wrote code which wardialled continually, then when the
morning operators came in they'd realize that there was no
data from the vending machines or whatever, and they'd
discover the hack really fast.

If you subvert one of these computers and interleave your
calls within the normal calls then nobody notices – not for
ages – and you can scan large areas that way. You could scan
the entire country in five years and no one would know. All this
stuff is out there waiting to be played with and no one seems
to realize it: they don't know, or they've forgotten that it exists.
They forget that new technology responds to old tricks.

Answerphones

T here was a time when hacking answerphones was the
latest craze. These things come in phases: these days
everyone's wireless network-crazy, but back then it was
answerphones. There were articles about hacking answerphones in *2600* and *PHUK* magazines. One day I was playing
around with a college phone system, manually wardialling
numbers to see what would happen. I managed to change the
outgoing answerphone message of the electrical engineering

department: I put on a Russian accent and changed it to. 'Please send your agents here for learning about electronics and hacking.' I left it there for a week or two, just to see what response I got.

Some people wouldn't leave a message, and others were just weird, but eventually the college figured it out and changed it back to a more sensible message. So I just changed it yet again to something else, and when they discovered the new message, I'd change it again. I played with their answerphone for quite a few weeks until I figured it was time to stop, but it was quite a harmless prank, really. It was a giggle, a little bit of fun, just a techno prank.

Another time I was dialling a friend, misdialled a digit and got connected to the PBX of a very large and well-known motoring organization. Of course, it wasn't office hours and they were closed, but I couldn't resist punching in some numbers and eventually got an outdial. Now I could dial up the PBX of the company and phone anywhere in the world I liked. For the next month, I used this PBX – I was even ringing up the DefCon voice bridge in the States – but eventually I decided that I'd used it enough.

I gave it out to a few friends; I think I even gave it to my father. Of course, eventually they realized the PBX was being abused and they fixed the problem, and there were no more free calls. People used to sell illegal PBX access, and that's just plain wrong. I found it and hacked it and used it for a while, and that was my reward for hacking it. It was wrong for me to use the PBX in the first place, but I tried not to abuse it too much. It was a big company, however, and I wouldn't want to abuse the PBX of a small company: they'd find it much harder to pay. That was the first PBX I ever hacked and I was really pleased with myself for being able to do it all on my own.

I've never done any blue-boxing. When I first started to go

to hacker meetings in 1993 or 1994, there were people around who were allegedly blue-boxing, but I didn't actually see it demonstrated until about 1996 or so. I didn't really see phones as anything much for playing around with – not unless you found a computer on the other end of the line.

I used to go 'Clark Kenting' with a laptop and an acoustic coupler in deserted phone boxes. I'd randomly wardial numbers by hand, and then I'd write down any computer modems I heard: then, when I went on a hacking spree, I'd go to local phone boxes in quiet, deserted areas and log into the computers I'd found. This was just after the Computer Misuse Act had come in, so what I was doing was illegal, but it was a lot of fun. That was the kind of thing I used to like doing when I was a hacker.

Something else I was doing at the same time was hacking voicemail boxes. Once again, I'd wardial by hand from phone boxes and when I found a voicemail system I'd hack out a couple of boxes. I didn't used to have a phone line back then and I couldn't afford a mobile, so I'd give out the number of the voicemail system to different people and they could get in touch with me that way. It was getting a bit silly, though: because people knew me really well from the local hacker meets I was getting all sorts of weird messages, so in the end I stopped hacking voicemail boxes completely.

Phreaking on TV

Do you remember the Channel Four programme about hacking which had a ridiculous sequence with these guys blue-boxing in Brighton using this huge beatbox? I heard through the grapevine that one of those guys had his house burnt down because they let the secret out. One person who might be interesting to talk to about that documentary would be M___: he seems to be tied into a lot of things. He was a member of the TKL hacker clan and they were really active, so he has a lot of contacts. It's rumoured that he has security clearance from the Government for the work he does in his day job, but that's just hacker rumours, and you can never trust hacker rumours. He always has loads of gadgets and stuff: he's highly skilled, but he can be paranoid. The first time I met him at a conference he was picking a lock, and I took a photograph of him and he was very scared about me having it, so I explained that I was P____ from London and that everyone knew me and trusted me and he was all right with that. I'm one of the few people in the hacker scene who can get away with taking photos of hackers because they trust me. I've taken a whole stack of photos of hackers doing things, and not just illegal things either, and they trust me to have them.

MOD phone snarf

I was active in the UK Phreaking scene between maybe 1995 and 2000. I used the handle M___, and hung about DAC, Dockmaster and a few other bulletin boards. I organized the Glasgow *2600* meeting, and just loved messing about with phones of all sorts.

Sometime around 2000, I allegedly cloned a mobile phone that I had allegedly 'snarfed'. The ESN I had allegedly used just happened to be an MoD cellphone: what are the chances of that happening? Very quickly, this resulted in MoD detectives turning up on my friend's doorstep with a search warrant. A few days later they turned up at my doorstep and searched my house. Nothing was found at my house, and a few friends and myself were questioned at the station.

I was put in the cells and questioned for a few hours. They

asked questions such as, 'Do you recognize this phone number?' and showed me the DAC BBS number. They asked me if I had ever heard of CompuLink – questions like that. Under the advice of a lawyer, I answered, 'No comment' to every question. I was released and informed a few weeks later that the Procurator Fiscal had decided that 'it was not in the public interest' to have me charged, and nothing more was heard of it.

I got a fright, and pretty much retired from playing with phones and BBSs. I still read alt.ph.uk now and again, but that's about all I do.

Telco engineers

I used to have Broadband connection – I became one of the phone company's test-monkeys and had a 1Mb connection, and it was wonderful. There was supposed to be, at worst, three-to-one contention, but I'm the only person in the area who has one, so there was no contention. I had a direct line to the Telco. I had the local cab box checked; the Telco engineer was really helpful. He explained how it all worked, how he used the 'beige box', everything.

Those Telco engineers are wonderful; they're so underpaid and bored that if anyone walks up to them and expresses an interest in what they're doing they will tell you in detail. They'll explain everything that's inside the cab box in intricate detail, how they test lines, what they do to trace lines, how their job control system works – everything. So in these cab boxes they have a little white box that you can just plug a normal phone in to, and just dial a '9' to get out, and the engineer explained all this to me. Of course, you could use somebody else's DP and a beige box with a set of croc-clips.

The easiest way was using an I-Phone, those little tiny two-inch-by-half-inch oval-shaped phones with buttons on them. All you did was plug one end into the socket, another bit into your earhole, and it had a little microphone. They were wonderful: splice in, use a couple of crocodile clips, one-two and you were away. You try buying one of them now! As soon as the authorities realized what they were being used for they were off the shelves like you wouldn't believe – they were gone. It was really infuriating.

These days, you can use the tone dial facility on mobile phones for DTMF dialling, and there are still 0500 and 0800 numbers that work. I don't know if there are any 'Country Direct' numbers out there now – there are still a lot of primitive phone systems out there, but I haven't looked for ages. There's still C5 all over the world, but these days they filter the lines to countries like Barbados so you can't break and seize the line.

Cable hack

One day, while a group of us were camped near a military airbase, we were digging a pit to use as a latrine when we came across this huge lump of copper wire. It was as thick as a man's arm: serious cable. We checked it for voltage and it was inert; no current or anything. We figured it had been put in there for years and was now obsolete and unused. We thought that if we dug it up for scrap nobody would even notice, because it was World War Two or Cold War cabling which was disused, so we hopped in through the airbase fence and borrowed a military JCB for a while. We drove right up the field for about 500 yards digging up this cable. It was so heavy we had to chop it into two-foot lengths to be able to lift it into the flatbed truck we'd brought with us. Then we zoomed off to the scrapyard and sold all this old copper cable, which we thought was left over from World War Two.

Not long after this, one day there was madness as all the sirens went off at once. Then all these aircraft zoomed over: there were all these crashes and bangs and smoke drifting. It turned out they were running a NATO exercise at the airbase, co-ordinating simulated air attacks from all over Europe to test their defence readiness. All these aircraft are simulating an attack on the airbase, and everything was cool, until at some point a referee must have decided that there had been a direct hit on the main power plant and that they would have to cut over to the emergency generator. When they cut to the emergency generator, there was an almighty bang as all the power on the airbase fused completely. The cable we'd uprooted and sold was the cable which ran from the emergency back-up generator. All that cable was coming from this large lumpy thing on the top of a hill with pipes sticking out of the top and a couple of manhole covers to allow access. They never figured out who had done it; they probably thought it was local kids. Maybe they assumed some tractor had ploughed through it, but we never got any follow-up on it; they never caught us.

Wi-fi prank

Wireless networks are still wide open; even now, years after the technology has been introduced. Even after all the warnings and horror stories in the media, it's still ridiculously easy to find a LAN to hop on to. This is a weakness in the knowledge of home users and companies, but you'd think that vendors and IT companies would know better, wouldn't you?

My favourite wireless network story comes from an IT

conference a few years back. Myself and a colleague were there for the day, and as usual we'd been round all the stands within an hour or two, had attractive women unusually fascinated by us and spoken to stand staff who didn't know their product from a hole in the ground. So the devil giving idle hands work to do meant my colleague started seeing what wireless networks were available.

Cobalt had brought out their RaQ recently and had a stand at the conference to show it off. My colleague and myself had evaluated the product, so we were familiar with how to get into it, the default logins, and a nice little program on the RaQ called 'lcdwrite', which could write any text to the 2x16 screen on the front of the device.

We sat in a convenient seat in the restaurant and we got into the Cobalt stand wireless network within a few minutes, and after a little longer we had Internet access through them, and had 'admin', the equivalent of root, on at least three of their RaQs. Of course, with the mission accomplished we didn't break anything; just made a few people laugh with little messages along the lines of

HELP I AM TRAPPED
IN A COBALT RAQ
ARE YOU BORED OF
THIS SHOW AS WELL?

Worryingly, I've heard of a similar situation at a security conference. My friend, a notorious member of the UK Digerati, was there and jumped on to a vendor's wireless LAN. The vendor was demonstrating a firewall technology and how it alerted you to incoming malicious traffic. My friend decided that was an appropriate time to throw lots of fun packets at the firewall's external interface, filling the demonstration screen with alerts while the speaker attempted to woo his conference-weary audience.

Country direct

B ecause I had access to JANET when I was at university, it wasn't until I became more involved in the hacker scene that I learnt about Phreaking. I'd read the theory and knew it used to be possible, but firmly believed that it wasn't any more. Then someone told me about 'Country Direct' lines and how they connected directly to C5 signalling systems in places like Cuba and Barbados.

Once I knew it was possible, I got my hands on a copy of 'Blue Beep' and a hand-held tape recorder. I knew the trunk might take some coaxing to seize, so I laid down a whole bunch of tests, varying the tones and timings a little bit to see if I got any luck.

I'd heard that the Telco monitors for Phreaking, so I'd wander off to another area code and try them out. Once I found a pattern of tones and times which worked, it would be back to the drawing-board and I'd make another tape with the tones necessary to dial through to a number. I'd pick the numbers from American magazines, or off the web. I didn't actually care who I was calling; I just wanted to see how far I could route the calls.

The thing was, once I'd worked out how to do it, it lost its appeal to me. I didn't see the point of prowling the streets looking for empty phone boxes just to make free calls, and I didn't like the idea that I was committing a serious crime, so I gave up blue-boxing.

It didn't stop me playing with phones, though. While we were waiting for the train to take us home from the monthly *2600* meetings, we used to while away the time doing hand scans of freephone numbers. We'd think up likely memorable combinations and then dial them and see what was at the other end: if it sounded like something interesting then we'd investigate later.

Wi-fi insecurity

I was testing a new design for an 802.11b antenna one night. Normally I get a WEP signal from the offices of a bank, and another WEP signal from a building across the road. I ignored these; if something's got a padlock, then I leave it alone. But then I found that a certain online retail organization had left its network wide open. I thought this was interesting and got curious. I did 'Network Neighbourhood' on the system and there were 276 computers, all of them totally and completely accessible. They were wide open, with full admin access for anyone to abuse. I found it quite frightening that a company like that should be so slack with its security. If I'd wanted to commit crime, I could have defrauded their systems for so much money by diverting goods and accessing their credit cards – but I'm not like that. I don't like to use my skills for crime.

These Wi-Fi networks are just open to abuse, and you don't have to be anywhere near the hot spot to access it. A 30-milliwatt card has a range of maybe 100 feet, but when you stick a 21dbi directional antenna on it, you're looking at 25 miles' range with a suitable receiver at the other end. With a satellite dish placed in front of a 21dbi directional antenna you can get a 75-mile range easily. I know there have been experiments with 12dbi antennae in America and they've got this kind of range. Every 3dbi is a doubling of power, so we're talking about a severe amount of power; we're talking about cooking pigeons if they get too close. So many systems aren't locked down; when war-walking or war-driving I find about

64 per cent of the systems aren't locked down with WEP. Only about a third of those are behind a firewall or have some kind of security to prevent you from browsing the network. I don't think the people who install these networks know what they're doing. They don't know that the moment you stick an antenna on an 802.11b card you up the range, so they forget to secure the networks.

I learned about aerials and antenna in the old CB radio days, where you had full-, half- and quarter-wave antennae. The larger your wave, the longer your aerial, and the longer your aerial, the more signal you could collect. An antenna focuses the radio wave – boosts it up – so the bigger the aerial, the longer the range. It gives more 'oomph': it works the same way as a reflector around the lightbulb in a torch. It's cheap and it's fun; the only restriction is that you need the line of sight to get a really good signal with these boosted antennae. If it could go through buildings, it'd be perfect.

Voicemail

I was in the mathematics teacher's office the other day and noticed an interesting little hack. I was sitting there and there was a phone, and on this phone there was a little label and it said, 'If there is an intermittent tone then you have voicemail. To go to voicemail dial "9000" and press "904#" followed by the password which is the same (904#)'. Now, I've seen this label before but never though much of it. I'm looking about a bit more and then I find three sheets of paper with all the internal and external numbers of the school.

So I looked up the mathematics department and looked up the teacher whose office it is and, sure enough, his number is 904! I thought, 'That was easy enough', so I got a copy of the list and now I can access everyone's voicemail.

It's a bit basic, but do you think that corporate or government phone security is any better? I wasn't intending on doing any hacking: I was just doing mathematics and then stumbled on it by accident.

Teletext

I don't know that there was a Prestel and Micronet community as such, but there always seemed to be more test and engineering pages than actual data.

Sometimes you'd come across a page with some Teletext-style art and a 'Kilroy Was Here' type of message, with no way to tell if this was a legitimate operator or had been left by some random hacker. Later, of course, it would transpire that an awful lot of people had gained access they weren't supposed to have.

Being a bit like a slightly more interactive version of Teletext, I got bored with it pretty quick. Other videotext-style systems weren't so lucky, though, especially since BBCs were so well adapted to accessing them. My way into these stemmed from a work placement I had where there was a VT terminal. I played with it a bit, found the dial-up number and access passwords stored on the machine in clear text, made a note of them and was off about my business.

Accessing the services available through the dial-in nodes was slightly harder, but with the four-digit ID/password combos, not *that* much more difficult. A typical examples would be getting into a flight reservations system. You would enter an ABTA merchant number as the ID. At that time, many ABTA agents displayed their merchant number on the shopfront, or in newspaper adverts, or often even in their advertisements in the Yellow Pages.

Micronet was kind of odd, and most of my time on there

was spent in this virtual 'Olde English pub', where everyone was deeply in character. It was kind of weird knowing all those other people were grown-ups who were paying out good money to hang out online and pretend to be Olde English knaves and wenches and suchlike. But then were they? Maybe they were all just pre-pubescent hackers.

BBSs: well, where do I start with that? I first started accessing BBSs at school via the BBC micros there. Eventually, after acquiring my first PC, I got a ropey 2400-baud modem and installed a wire under the carpet in our house so that I could access BBSs from home. It was a bit like following a trail of crumbs, really: one BBS would yield a hacking file which would have another, groovier, more hacker-oriented board listed in its fileid.diz file, and so on, and so forth.

I was never a regular on any hacking-specific BBSs, largely because even then I was conscious of getting busted, or in trouble at least: but I was a regular on a board called Drealm, on which I spent many happy, and often drunken, hours in the years before emigrating to university.

Trashing

Black bag operation

There was one particular office belonging to a local cable provider which did Internet access and phones. We always wanted to trash them because they were the local cable company and we knew that almost everyone in the area used them.

The only problem was that every time we went near the place, the security was as tight as a drum. You could see the trash bins in the car park, but there was a locked gate and, worse still, a little cabin where the security guard sat.

We'd almost given up when we were driving past one day in a car belonging to a non-hacker and noticed the gate was open and there were no security guards present. Much to our friend's surprise, we demanded that he stop the car. As soon as it came to a halt, G____ and I hot-footed it across the car park, grabbed as many likely-looking black bags as possible, then legged it back to the car as quickly as possible.

The look on our friend's face as we piled back into the car with all these bags of rubbish was hilarious. When we went through the trash, the contents were a goldmine: internal circuit numbers, memos, procedures, loads of stuff. The best bit was the customer service sheets; they had details of reference numbers, client bank accounts, home addresses and telephone numbers. If we'd been criminals, we could have abused that information, but we chucked it away. We were just after the technical information.

Another time we found a City dealing room which was being modernized. It was full of VT-100 terminals, terminal servers and these weird serial networking boxes. G___ and I had to make three car trips in his station wagon to get them all home. We had so many phones that we were giving them away to friends for months. G___ pulled out a telephone exchange and took it home and installed it, and I think the serial network boxes became the core of his home control system.

As for the rest of it, my entire computer room is furnished from trashing. I haven't had to buy any desks, shelves, swivel chairs or anything. I haven't bought a phone or a computer for years, but I'm surrounded by computers. My son's stereo is a neat Sony mini-system I found while trashing. It's so easy to pick computers off the street and recycle them; even old Pentium IIs make great Linux servers. If they're too old, I just scrap them and recycle the parts. I like the trashing aspect of hacking because it's a very pro-active way to recycle the junk which would normally go into a landfill, and it means I don't have to spend as much money on computers. I can get all the technology I need to feed my habit without breaking the bank.

Brush with the law

I've been out trashing with quite a few hackers. One of them was Y___, who used to have a reputation as Trasher King. Every time he dived into a skip, he'd come out with something interesting. Nowadays, V___ seems to be the Trasher King, I think because he's more active and lives in a good area for computer trashing.

One day, Y____ and I were trashing a skip near the Civil Aviation Authority and fished out a whole load of 486 servers – big ones that looked like R2D2 units from *Star Wars*. Y____ had just the right equipment to transport these server units: a couple of skateboards. So we stacked these units on to the skateboards and wheeled them away to O___'s workshop in Aldwych. We managed to get six or so computers out of the skip that day.

The thing is that I've been trashing since before I heard the term. I didn't realize that what I was doing was trashing. I used to live round the corner from a computer shop, and the owner used to get software for reviews. Because he couldn't sell the software once he'd reviewed it, he used to chuck it out in the bin, so I figured out that if I went down to the rubbish bins the day before the rubbish came and grabbed the black bags from his shop, I might get some new games and posters and whatever. It was pretty good, but I told a few friends about this and we were soon in a competition to see who could get the bags first, but without getting there too early. The owner eventually noticed that his rubbish was being removed before the dustman arrived, so he figured it out.

I went out trashing after a hacker meeting with someone who'd never been trashing before, so we went up to Oxford Street and spotted a whole pile of computer boxes, which is always a good sign: there could be unused software, manuals, old computers – anything, really – but it looked like someone had got there first. I was with this young guy called X___; he's a very strange creature. He's a stereotypical hacker, very shy, very quiet. I think he speaks in computer code, a bit like R2D2; he bleeps instead of talking, which can be very amusing sometimes. He's a very strange guy, but I accept him because he's a part of the hacker crowd. He'll probably come out of his shell later on in life, but the most I ever heard him speak was when this girl came down to the hacker meeting to see him especially: he managed about three words that night.

While X___ was rummaging around in the trash, some of the other hackers noticed that there was a police van taking an interest, so they wandered off and made themselves scarce. This meant X___ was the one who caught trying to climb out of the skip very, very slowly, as though he could make himself invisible by moving slowly. Of course, the police were watching all this thinking, 'What's he doing?' and taking more of an interest than they normally would. I'm hiding behind the skip, and I didn't think they could see me, or that they'd see me even if they got out of the car, because there was a place to hide. The big problem was that I couldn't let X___ get busted because he doesn't speak at all, and I knew he would have problems when they started to ask him what he was doing. I had this vision of X___ bleeping and the police just picking him up and sectioning him, or something. Being a social engineer, and a bit of a clown, I put on my clown's nose – I keep a clown's nose in my pocket. So I put the nose on, and when the police asked X___ what he was doing I popped up from behind the skip saying, 'I think he's looking for a place to sleep'. The police were totally shocked because I'd just popped out of nowhere. They didn't know what to do: there they were, dealing with these two nutters – and then we had a stroke of luck. They had an emergency call somewhere else and just said, 'Pick up the rubbish and we'll be back to check in 20 minutes.' Of course, I just played the gent and agreed, so X___ and me started to pick up the rubbish, but as soon as the police vanished we quickly left. We thought it was a close call; but being a clown and a social engineer can get you out of trouble sometimes.

Tinsel trash

There's this very large local shopping mall where lots of people come and it has lots of secret passages. They're great: I love urban exploration. I used to go down there trashing, and one time I took a guest down there to show him around and do some trashing. Normally there's this old security guard there who just drinks and sleeps in his little hut, but this time there was a temporary security guard who went mental. This guy was huge – massive – and very keen, shouting and waving his arms around, so we acted stupid, like we were looking for the multi-storey car park, and kept asking for directions. When he calmed down, we started talking to him and he gave us a guided tour of the underground sections of the mall. It was cool. These huge security guards get the jobs because they look big and scary, but when you start talking to them they can be socially engineered like everyone else.

On another occasion I spotted a complete shop till as well as the normal computer junk, so I picked it up and shoved it into a box, but there was a lot of it and it was heavy and the box was rubbish. I went out and looked for a piece of string to tie the bits together. There were police at the front of the mall and they wanted to know what I was doing and I told them and offered to show them the underground passages at the mall. They were up for this and I took them on a guided tour of the underground passages until they realized that their radios didn't work. Then they headed back to the car; but they weren't worried about us trashing at all. The funny thing was that when we left the mall there was a huge six-foot-long piece of golden tinsel stuck to my backside, so there I was crossing this main road with a box full of an old till and computer gear, trying not to look too conspicuous, and I didn't realize about the tinsel trailing behind me.

Hacker Culture

Conferences

I've been to the US conferences H2K in 2000, Beyond HOPE in 2001 and HAL in Holland in 2001. I also went to all three of the UK Access All Areas conferences in 1995, 1996 and 1997, and also DNS in Blackpool. I've never been to BrumCon, but I have been to a lot of other hacker parties and gatherings.

I think it was in 1996 we had the hacker party: in 1995 I wasn't invited because I wasn't elite enough, but in 1996 I was, and that was good. The party was held somewhere in C_____ in the upstairs room of a pub. Emmanuel Goldstein, the editor of *2600* magazine, had to catch an early flight but didn't want to stay at the airport overnight because it would have been boring, so he decided to stay at the party as long as we promised to get him to the airport on time. That was when I first met Emmanuel Goldstein and started chatting to him and getting to know him. The only way to get him to the airport on time was for him to abseil out of the window of the pub. People like P_____ and J_____ were holding on to the rope and G_____ 'just happened' to have some abseiling kit in his bag.

The only guy Emmanuel trusted enough was me, because

the only one who was sober enough to make a judgement on whether it was feasible was me. This was because I'd met him earlier, introduced myself, showed him this article about Emmanuel and asked him to sign it. I asked him for his signature because he's one of my heroes and he was surprised and flattered. Then he said, 'Oh, but you're in this article, too; you're as famous as me.' I'm not, of course – I was just a little mention in a whole A3 page – but that's how I met him. So I managed to convince him that it would be safe to let these guys hold on to the rope while he abseiled down. I taped it on video and showed it at a conference with the *Mission Impossible* theme playing over the top of it. The great thing was that just as his feet touched the ground the taxi turned up, so he managed to catch his plane back to America on time.

HAL in Holland in 2001 was really good. It was a very relaxed atmosphere; maybe too relaxed, because I'm not the best person at getting up in the morning. It was great to see Rop Gongrijp again, because I hadn't seen him since Access All Areas in 1993. The Dutch and other Europeans are really friendly and welcoming. There were some really good talks, on the psychology of hacking, social engineering and technical workshops. The Chaos Computer Club had a big tent and were teaching lock-picking, so I really got into lock-picking at that time. It was just very relaxed compared to the *2600* conferences in New York, because they tend to be in hotels and conference venues and there isn't so much freedom. Also with the free flow of cannabis in Holland it's like an expansion of minds and everyone talks very freely, so even if later on you realize that you were talking complete rubbish, it doesn't matter. It's good fun, but I do like conferences and I'm a very sociable person on the hacking scene, even though I can be very shy in real life. I know most of the people in the hacker scene these days whom I've got to know over the years.

The other major difference between the HAL and HOPE is that the talks seemed more organized in New York, so if you wanted to learn things instead of meeting people, then the *2600* conferences would be the place to go: they tend to be more rigid. You couldn't get up to so much because you had hotel security around, so there wasn't so much tinkering, whereas at HAL people tinkered with computers a lot. But you have to remember that most of the hacker history is based in America, and the major hackers are from America. You've got Captain Crunch walking around, Emmanuel Goldstein, people like that, and Kevin Mitnick on the end of a telephone line talking to us from prison. Next year I want to go to HOPE and meet Kevin Mitnick: he's another one of my heroes. I feel he was treated very unfairly, and that's putting it mildly: he got a really bad deal. People made a lot of money out of Kevin Mitnick and he went to prison because of it.

It's always good to go to a hacker conference because you put faces to handles, you make more friends and you learn lots of new stuff. You wander off with someone and you learn some lock-picking techniques or you meet someone else and learn new exploits, or whatever. It's definitely worth going to if you've never been: educational and fun at the same time.

Hacking tools

A hacking tool is a systems administrator's tool in the wrong hands. It's like a crowbar. You can buy a crowbar for opening packing cases or lifting floorboards, but you can also use it for breaking down someone's door. It's the purpose you use the tool for which makes you a good or a bad person. So if anyone asks why I've got all these hacking tools on my system, then my answer is 'So what?' I haven't got a phone line so I'm not connected to the Internet at home, so I can't be hacking anything. I've got a home network and the only systems I hack using these tools belong to me, so unless they can arrest me for hacking my own systems I'm not doing anything illegal.

The reason why I hack into my own systems is to learn where they're vulnerable, so that I can protect myself and advise other people. Not having a phone line means that I can never be accused of hacking and I'm never going to get hacked. Not connecting a home network to the Internet is the best way of guaranteeing that you won't be hacked: that's the ultimate in computer security.

Elitism

I'm just a bog-standard hacker, funnily enough. I was at a *2600* meeting and I met this young guy and introduced myself and he was surprised. He said that he thought I'd be some kind of elite *über*-hacker and there I was in the flesh, and I wasn't like that. I told him I was just an ordinary, common-or-garden computer enthusiast, someone who loved playing with and exploring the technology for its own sake. The fact that I've been doing it for years doesn't make me elite; it doesn't make me anything, right? It's just an attitude that hackers have, and I seem to have it, and that makes me a hacker, but it doesn't make me elite.

All that elite stuff really annoys me. Instead of sharing knowledge, there's all this hierarchy and one-upmanship. People who should be on the scene sharing knowledge and teaching people things that they don't understand play these elite games, and they say, 'Oh, I can't tell you that; you're not elite enough.' What kind of rubbish is that? It's madness. What do I have to learn to be elite enough that you're going to share information with me? How can I prove I'm elite enough for you? Anyway, 99 per cent of this so-called elite knowledge isn't even interesting. It can be really, really esoteric, just aimed at a small field, and if you aren't into that kind of hacking it isn't worth it.

What really impresses me is really good hacks: stuff that is novel, interesting and technologically advanced; stuff that make you think. The work that's been done recently by H____ in activating Windows frames and buttons in the Novell administration tool NWAdmin – that's a great hack. It's a very powerful tool, and just knowing that it can be done makes me aware of a lot of problematic issues in network administration. I don't know enough about Windows internals to write a program like that, but just knowing that someone can peek into the WIN32 API like that, and subvert normal system permissions, makes me very alert. It means a tool which would normally be in a public directory, one which people are meant to use to change their personal details, isn't safe. Once I know this, I can make sure the administration tool is taken out of the public directory and put somewhere where only someone with admin privileges can use it. It might inconvenience the users, but it makes the system much safer, because it turns out that the system administration tool itself was a security risk.

Now I've learned that the technique exists, I start to wonder; how many other network administration tools using the WIN32 API can be subverted in the same way? I've started to wonder if certain Active Directory management tools can be exploited in the same way, because if you can use that technique to subvert those tools, no corporate network is safe. It's a cutting-edge technique, and once you think through the implications, the ramifications are potentially huge. If I knew more about WIN32 API and C++, I'd be exploring this sort of thing right now: it has great potential for the future.

I think in the early days I followed the hacker stereotype: a loner, an explorer, not very good with girls at the time because I looked too young for my age and no one took me seriously. I get fed up with the stereotype of the hacker as a social misfit and loner; it's boring, it's a cliché and it's just not true. If you put a bunch of hackers in a room and give them a catalyst to break the ice, beer or cannabis or whatever, then once they get talking there's no stopping them. It's the same as any other social group: once everyone's had as much of their preferred social lubricant as they need, the room ignites.

Hacker

There was this hacker conference: I think it was H2K, but it might have been as early as 1989. Hacking must have been the 'in' thing that year, because there were a lot of TV programmes reporting it. Channel Four were making a TV programme about hackers. They wanted to make a documentary and I explained to them that they'd get a better documentary if they filmed in New York, because it was the home of *2600* magazine and Emmanuel Goldstein would be there. What they wanted was good television: something that wouldn't get them into trouble, or us either. So I sold them on the concept of going to New York to H2K, which was great. I was liasing with the documentary team and the UK hackers because we thought they were planning to make a documentary about the UK hackers, including me, so a load of UK hackers and I went over to New York to be part of this documentary – to get to be on TV talking about hacking. We thought this was great. So we got to the conference in New York and I started asking around for the documentary team, explaining that I was meant to meet them, and someone said 'They're here already in the main hall.' So I went and found them and they weren't the people I was expecting; they were a young man and woman. I ambled up to start talking to them and asking about my contacts at Channel Four, and they were baffled: they knew nothing about it. It turned out they were another film crew from Channel Four who knew nothing at all about our documentary. There were two teams making documentaries for Channel Four. Later, the woman admitted I had actually scared her when we first met: I think the clown's nose didn't help, I use my clown's nose all the time for ice-breaking and social engineering.

We managed to get drunk in a local bar with all the hackers, had a great time and then moved on to the dance floor. Later on, I wondered if I was cheating, using my social-engineering skills to chat up this woman. I was hacking a person and it seemed a little unfair. Other people just call it flirting, but the end result was the same: I think it's called penetration testing.

The next day I had to give a talk: I had to get back to where I was staying miles away and get ready for a panel about 'The International Hacking Scene.' This place was like a Hackers' HQ in Manhattan and it was where some of the hackers were staying. A lot of hackers tended to sleep there during conference: we'd all slept there the year before for Beyond HOPE as well. At that conference I was treated like royalty. I'd been invited over by Emmanuel Goldstein to come over and do some talks, I didn't have to pay anything and I even got picked up at the airport. So the first time in New York was great: I met Emmanuel, Cheshire Catalyst and a few others. It was like a hacker pilgrimage to see my childhood heroes.

The second time in New York was a bit of a let-down. I made my own way from the airport, had hardly any money and couldn't contact anyone because I'd left my numbers at home due to bad planning, so meeting this woman while in New York was a result, especially as everyone was chasing this girl after she'd done a TV programme about the M___ hacking crew.

The original TV crew, even though they filmed us all at the conference and in London, eventually did the TV programme at DefCon rather than H2K. They thought it was more 'Hollywood'. I'd been walking around the conference with a Union flag as a cape, like I was Captain Britain or something, representing the hackers from the UK by literally 'flying the flag'. They didn't use the New York footage, they didn't use the London footage, they used the Las Vegas footage, and they didn't even bother to tell us that they were going to. We never heard a word from them: they never apologized or anything.

I think it was at H2K that someone tried to organize an orgy and got busted by the FBI because they thought there might be paedophiles or something. Only about four people turned up, a couple who only wanted each other and a couple of gay guys, and they all got arrested. Then when someone threw a firecracker out of a window it was exaggerated by the press into a stick of dynamite, which was a shame, because part of the roof of the hotel opposite fell on to someone the next day.

Identity crisis

There was a time a little while back where I had an identity crisis: I couldn't justify calling myself a hacker because I wasn't actively hacking any more. There are a lot of people out there who have more knowledge than me, but I was in the right place in the right time. I met Emmanuel Goldstein, got a '2600.com' account and have been coming to the meetings for so long that I was like an unofficial leader. I tried to liaise with the Americans on stuff about certain things which might be important, like when we had criminals coming down to the meetings. I knew this was bad, but we can't stop them coming down because it's a public meeting. Whenever we had problems which concerned me enough to get in touch with Emmanuel for advice – things like the protest at the American Embassy – he appreciated that we did that and he wanted to include it on the *Freedom Downtime*[9] DVD.

Somewhere I've got the photos of that protest, but I'm not that bothered about them going on the DVD: it was something I did because I related to Kevin Mitnick. I don't really need any credit for it; it's just a piece of hacker history, that's all. Emmanuel's spoken to me on several occasions; he knows what I've done, he knows where I'm coming from and he knows why I did it. He knows I have that mental attitude that I call hacker spirit. I've been in the London scene for so long that I've seen the scene change, from good times to bad, and now it's starting to come back again.

The hacker scene has changed: it used to be really great in 1993–94, but it went downhill and hasn't really recovered. There were a lot of very knowledgeable people on the scene at that time and a lot of things going on. I'm still there helping out with the London scene, helping out the younger hackers, making sure they don't get involved in criminal activities, giving guidance and information to anyone who wants it.

---

[9] *Editor's note*: *Freedom Downtime* is a full-length documentary about the campaign to free Kevin Mitnick and the hacker world. See www.freedom-downtime.com for more details.

As for the future, these days I'm interested in wireless hacking. There's going to be a lot more hacking of 802.11b and Bluetooth. There's a great new tool out for hacking Bluetooth, and more and more it just looks like an open invitation for anyone to read confidential documents sent from computers to printers, or data from phone to pda, or even voice conversations. Now I hear about Blue-Jacking, where people are sending anonymous messages to people's Bluetooth kit and driving them nuts. People don't realize that it isn't safe, but when you've grown up being a bit of a computer whiz kid then you look at things in a different way.

Toolbox

Tools like hex editors and techniques like that are good to learn. I remember at school they had a Nimbus computer network. The central server was in the same room and they stored the passwords on a 70K floppy disk in this server. Because I'd learnt DOS commands I used to wait until the teacher was out of the room and then I copied the password disk. As an infiltration hacker, I learned early on in life that when you went into a place it was good to have a lot of disks with you. Then when you found interesting information, or interesting programs, or anything interesting, you'd take a copy of it. You'd take it home and put in your PC and then dissect it at home, run the programs and figure out how they worked. Then you'd know more the next time you came back. I also learned to build up a box of floppy disks, which I called my toolkit. I had a program called 'fwl', which was a file transfer program which also allowed you to read the first few pages of a text file and to change into directories – even hidden directories. These used 'hi-ascii' ALT keys to build directories which were useful to protect things. I think it was

'ALT-254' to create a box in DOS, but in Windows it came up like an underscore so you could click into it.

Computer art

I did a computer art exhibition once – one of the first Internet computer art exhibitions ever. We even got BT to sponsor it. It was part of their drive to test what was the 'brand-new' Internet service, so we hooked up with Apple computers and BT and went off to this exhibition.

The exhibition was in the Serpentine Gallery and the biggest exhibit was a huge pile of secondhand clothes. You had to bring a plastic bag and take clothes home with you so they were all gone by the end of the evening. It was called 'Take Me, I'm Yours'. We set up an Internet connection in the entrance lobby and built a little catalogue for the exhibition. It would be pretty standard stuff now, but in those days only the Louvre in Paris had a website: even the National Gallery didn't have one.

Because the exhibition was called 'Take Me, I'm Yours', we got a copy of the tune by Squeeze and looped that around and around. We had to limit access to 15 minutes on the computer, so all these people went round this exhibition in about five minutes: then they spent 15 minutes playing with the Internet. It was cool. BT were sponsoring the exhibition, before they were offering any sort of IP service, and they even gave us the server space for the website.

Nintendo generation

There's a lack of focus in this country: something defi-nitely needs to be done. I remember in the early Nineties, there were things happening. You had the analogue cellular stuff, Sky encryption cards getting cracked, all the pager stuff going on. Now it seems to be more rigid and less experimental. The 1980s were when computing first started for me, but by the 1990s we had what I call the Nintendo Generation, where people were getting games consoles and not actually programming and learning about computer hardware, because all they had to do was stick in a cartridge and play a game, and that was all they wanted to do. Not many people would take them apart to find out how they worked and you couldn't reprogram them because there was no BASIC built in, so you couldn't play around so much.

Computing magazines took on a different focus. The old Sinclair magazines used to have program listings, circuit diagrams and projects to make, like your own light pen – all sorts of things – and you just don't get those in mainstream computer magazines any more. The magazines just reflect computers as consumer products rather than technological toys; they make computers easier by dumbing down the information required to operate them. There aren't many people these days who'd buy a Furby and take it apart, modify it, add a computer interface and rebuild it so that it was better than before[10].

When I have children I intend to invest in a really large Lego set, especially the robot kits and a computer interface. This is what was around in the Sixties: you had Lego and Meccano and the German stuff I can't remember the name of. You had all this stuff that you could create things with, and now you just get some toy that's packaged and ready-built for you, with TV tie-ins and stuff. It doesn't stretch the imagination and creativity so much.

[10] *Editor's note*: Anyone who is interested in modifying their Furby should see: www.homestead.com/hackfurby

The future

I think hacking has a future. It's an aggressive subcultural meme that just won't go away. For every time I've heard or seen someone complain that hacking's dead, there's a case to contradict them.

In an increasingly systems-oriented world, I reckon more and more people, particularly those in fields outside computing, will pick up on the 'systems mindset'. Also, it seems to me that not only does modern technological culture provide a nurturing environment of sorts for the hacker meme; it actively requires hackers in order to survive and make progress.

In terms of tech, the next big thing is always going to be – well, the next shiny new thing that comes along.

If asked, I'd have to say that the interesting stuff for future hackers is going to be:

(The anonymous contributor puts on a 'Prophet of Doom' voice.)

ID theft. On the rise and becoming a serious problem, it relates to the problem of criminal hackers below. I think this will get worse before it gets better: from what I've read recently, NHTCU et al are running to keep up.

Criminal hackers. Organized crime influences will suborn script kiddies and other hackish types.

Sooner or later, they will come. If there's money in it and it's illegal, they'll be there eventually. For all I know, it's happening already. I hope not. I hope the natural distrust that hackers seem to have built in will help out, but I know there are people out there just dying for the opportunity. Let's hope they don't have to.

When Worms Attack! Virii, worms and other malware seem to be increasing and, more worryingly, the rate of increase also seems to be rising. Already it's getting so that you can't go anywhere on the web without someone attempting to foist some kind of spyware on you. Virii and worms are rampant. After years of virtually virus- and worm-free computing, my Minesweeper is now stopping up to 30 emails per day containing virii, and just the other day I saw a nasty worm infestation at an organization which thought it was patched up.

Spam Wars. Don't you just hate spam? Recent stats suggest that the percentage of bulk mail is increasing. Spammers are even resorting to using worms and Trojans to do their dirty work for them now. This crossover between the virus writer and spam communities is genuinely disquieting, suggesting worse to come, and also suggesting that the aggression level is going to rise. With spammers playing dirty, and systems administrators and anti-spam activists deploying more aggressive tools to catch spammers and put a crimp in their activities, we should be able to see some serious sparks flying before too long.

Cyber-Apocalypse Now. Sooner or later, the one thing we all fear will happen. Someone will come along who has not only the ability but also the motivation and the will to produce a cyber 9/11.

I tend not to pry around critical infrastructure in case I break it, but it seems increasingly clear from recent events that critical infrastructure around the world is vulnerable to attack. God knows, people have been worrying about this since before I was born and it hasn't happened yet, as far as we know; but one day, it almost certainly will.

The War Against Hackers: Of course, given the above, this must surely follow: Operation Sundevil on a global scale – except probably much less effective, given the state of global co-operation at the moment.

Hactivism: As more and more hackers get thoroughly fed-up with the state of the world, they will engage in some form of 'hactivism'. By this I mean anything from defacing corporate and government websites to setting up and maintaining contact databases for their local Friends of the Earth or Greenpeace cell. This can surely only be A Good Thing.

Hackers' Tales

Why hack?

'**H** ack. Hack because you can, because you want to, because you know deep, deep down that it's not even who you are; it's *what* you are.'

Dumbhost ISP

I t all started on A___'s 19th birthday when we decided to drink as much beer as possible and own as many websites as possible. We had an account on the Dumbhost servers, so we used a Server Side Include (SSI) exploit, which is a piece of computer code designed to exploit security holes in a web server.

We got it from some Chinese website and it actually had to be run through Google translation services to get a working program back out of it. We cut and pasted it, ran it through Google and changed a couple of the brackets, which obviously weren't English.

We ran it, and it 'shells off' the command you give it. It will shell off from Apache, because Apache uses this SSI thing: when the exploit shells off, it gives you access to any command you like. Because Apache doesn't run as 'nobody' but as 'apache', the 'apache user', it means that it has access to all the virtual hosts on the server.

We thought this was a prime target, and the account we had was literally full up. There must have been about 15 reseller accounts in there, and then we found a couple more we had access to which had three or four hundred reseller accounts. If we could access these, we'd have so many websites we could access and drop files on to, so we basically uploaded the SSI hack, which allowed us to run commands on the server and feed back through Internet Explorer. It would give you directory listings, or execute whatever command you gave it.

We found it quite funny to change the code on the script a bit and make it look like the Windows XP browser. We could get files, download files or view files in the browser. We generated a PHP script, which created a directory listing, and if you pressed the 'get' link it would grab the file and pipe it down to your machine. It would use content definition headers in the HTML to treat it like an email attachment and then start to download the file to the machine by piping it through the PHP script.

Obviously, there's a 'HOME' directory, and the prefix was the first two letters of the username, just like every website. Once you were in that directory there was a list of all the usernames, and when you went into those directories you found the public HTML directory, and once you got in there, you'd got all their HTML.

That's what they get access to: they get into there via ftp and that's it. There was also a logs directory and also QMAIL mailboxes for dumping all the mail in. I have to mention this: PHP MyAdmin is a hacker's best friend. The website owners use it to administer their database.

The first thing we found on one of these resellers'

accounts was a computer supplier with a PHP config file, so we viewed the PHP config file using our nice script, then copied out the plain text password and username. Then we went into our local PHP MyAdmin, put the username and password into there and got into the customer's database.

It dumped their entire database because we were connected to them. We went into the prices table and found a £3,000 ($5,000) tablet PC. We thought it was really funny to change the price to £4.99 for about 10 minutes, and then we got scared and changed it back. We took a screen shot of the specifications page of this tablet PC, made by Toshiba, and dumped it on the web server, and that kind of stuff.

One of the users had backed up his username and password in a plain text file, and this was the real goal. We took that file and then logged in. We had a reseller account with about 1,200 resold accounts and we went through the first 50 adding a little PI symbol to the website in the bottom right-hand corner. I don't know how many websites we hit that night, but it was lots.

I thought about PHP. They hadn't put any restrictions on PHP, and obviously that was the reason we were able to do this, so we had a look around and found we could open socket connections. Then we scanned the local IP address range, 192.168.0.1-255. Suddenly we found we'd resolved the internal domain name for all the given machines – including office.dumbhost.co.uk. We just had a look in this server.

Once we knew the open ports, we decided to do an HTTP request to each of the ports and hosts in turn, using the open socket connection, and then it would return whatever it got back. The banner might say it was a Cisco or whatever and 'please log in', and a couple of them with prefix 'gw' gateways were Cisco routers.

We went back to the office machine and the port 80 was

open, and it was running a local web host – IIS, I think – so we had a look at that server and wrote a script to view those files and get a directory listing. We found things like 'cisco-passwords.txt' with the instructions, 'This updates weekly – please review this every week', which was quite useful. We found quite a few other things, like how they calculated their bandwidth and which users were reselling accounts. Things like this are really handy to know.

Labour party

I always enjoyed myself when I went to the hacker parties in M____, which were run allegedly by F___ and his PHP crew, people like, G____, J____ and S____. If there was anyone else who used to help out, I'm sorry that I can't remember your names, but you know who you are.

These parties used to be really good: they'd have music, and people would bring kit with them to play with and sit round and chat and drink. The worst thing about those parties was that there would be an elite room, like a VIP lounge, and trying to get into that was a big challenge, especially for an infiltrator hacker like myself, but it's something I've always managed to do. In fact, there's a great story that comes to mind. I'll tell you and then you can sanitize it the best you can.

It was in 1996 or 1997. I think there were three parties in M___ and I think they were Controversy in 1996, Conspiracy in 1997 and Catastrophe in 1999. I think Conspiracy was in the middle and it was the time that the Labour Party was trying to get into power. Allegedly the TKL crew had hacked the Liberal Party website, so we watched S___ in the elite room trying to hack a website which just happened to be the Labour Party web page. One night, while S___ was trying to hack this website, he managed to get root access, so he owned the site, but he didn't do anything with the access. He got root access – total control of the Labour Party web page – and we were hoping there'd be lots of media coverage in the Sunday papers, but nothing was really reported.

A group of us decided that, as a publicity stunt, it would be good to do something to the Labour Party web page. S____ wasn't interested in doing anything, but J____ worked the terminal in some cybercafe and decided on the Spitting Image graphic. We told loads of people that we were going to do it: G___, P___ and another guy called O___ were involved. We all came from London, and we were driven up to M___ by G___. I got to know G___ really well at that time: it was great. Nowadays G___'s a really good mate I've got to know when doing road trips to places like M___.

It didn't take long for the hack to be done and J___ had doctored the images for the web page. Once we got back to London the graphics and everything were all ready and we were going to start with a big press announcement to be released on the Monday. I was chosen with O___ as the best social engineers to phone up the press agencies and announce that we'd hacked the web page and that we were big bad hackers and we'd do loads more stuff etc. It was just meant to be a little prank to get into the press, a little stunt that wasn't designed to hurt anyone and would actually probably give more publicity to the Labour Party website than any of us lot, especially as election year was due.

Eventually I was the only one speaking to the press agencies, because O___ couldn't carry on: he was getting freaked out by all the questions that they kept asking him, so it was down to me to carry on chatting to the press with all my different accents. I started alternating the calls to the press agencies, I told them anything they wanted to hear: that we were badass hackers, cyber-terrorists, anything to get publicity for the web page hack. Certain companies didn't want to get involved, like ITN and some of the other news companies, but the BBC took it: I find that they're a very good channel and very independent. We said we were going to hack more pages and stuff like that, but it was no big deal as far as we were concerned.

The only problem was that J___ had credited the hack to the PHP group: I think there's a copy of the hacked web page in the *2600* website, and this wasn't so good because it pissed the Government off, so the Government went for the PHP members in a big way. They knew that F___ was a part of this group and he was really fed-up that the hack had been credited to this group, because he was having his own problems with busts for hacked web pages and cellular hacking. So the police started arresting people like F___, and S___. They finally managed to arrest J___ just by association, and that wasn't good because he was having problems with the police anyhow because this arsehole called O___ had managed to get a lot of people in trouble. O___ used to hang around calling himself D___, but he was just pretending to be elite: in reality he was just a lamer. I knew him for a while but luckily dropped him like a hot potato before he got me into any trouble.

So they did all these arrests: the police arrested F___ with MP5 machine-guns, broke into his house in the wee small hours, dragged him away and interrogated him. J___ was going to be prosecuted for it: they couldn't actually prove that he'd done it, but the other case put him in the frame. Eventually the only people who got away without any problems and escaped the wrath of justice were G___ who got out of town before all this happened, and of course me, who was from London.

It made *Computer Weekly*, and it was still being brought

up in many magazines about hacked web pages with the same graphics until very recently. J___ didn't actually get charged, but funnily enough I heard that one of the reasons he wasn't prosecuted was because his uncle was a Labour Lord and the Labour Government didn't want any scandal – but that's just another hacker rumour: more likely they didn't have enough evidence to charge him.

That's one of the major things I've been involved in. I didn't actually do the hacking myself as such, but that's because I don't hack computers so much, I'm much more of a people hacker.

X___, who is into all sorts of Government-type things, and allegedly has Government security clearance, actually informed me recently that the Government is still looking for the Labour Party website hackers, because they really want a prosecution.

As for the technical details, I think it was a SunOS type hack, but it gave them root access, so it was some kind of Unix system. As I say, I wasn't involved in the hack itself; just the PR around it. We're talking 1996 or 1997, so it would have been an old-school operating system, not one of the newer ones like W2K or XP, but it might have been NT4.0 and they got admin access instead. Either way they owned the machine and had total control over it, but those kinds of techie details can be boring in a way. Once you 'own' someone else's machine it doesn't matter what operating system you run; the computer does what you want and might as well be sitting on your desk.

Unwanted backdoors

I was working for an organization as a contractor, and I was in the computer room checking out the systems when I

found that the SPARC Solaris system, which ran their membership database, had a mysterious serial cable coming out the
back. So I tracked it back and found a modem attached to this
serial cable, and attached to the modem was a live phone line.
These guys had attached their membership system to the
public switched telephone system, and I couldn't believe it.
Anyone who scanned the area code where the organization
was located could have found this modem and hacked into
their system, and they didn't seem to care. The system even
announced itself nicely: the banner said it was a Solaris system
and who owned it and even what it did. What a target! It would
have been so easy for any decent hacker to hack into that box.
It might as well have had a sign saying, 'Please hack me.'

So I went back to the IT department and asked someone
what the phone number was and they gave it to me.
Everyone knew the number to this system, so I looked
around the people I'd been introduced to that week and
isolated one person who I knew supported Arsenal football
team and was enthusiastic about football. I fired up my PC
and dialled the modem upstairs and logged in as that user
with the password 'Arsenal' within five minutes. I freaked out
and went to my boss and demanded that the modem was
disconnected. I told her all about what I'd just found and she
wasn't happy. At least she understood IT security, not like the
other people in the organization. Later on, we found out that
a Unix consultancy company was using the dial-in line to
check whether the backups had finished or not, so we
stopped all that and removed all access from outside. Just
finding and fixing that phone line made the company more
secure: then, getting rid of the consultants and checking the
backups in-house saved the company a whole pile of money.
That's one of the benefits of employing a hacker with a
decent moral and ethical code.

Even though I have an ethical code, if I'd thought to scan this area code before I worked for the company and found that server, I'd have hacked it. I would have made every effort to hack their SPARC server and their membership database: it would have been a seriously high-profile hack as well. But once they were paying me to look after and secure their systems, I had no choice but to pull the plug on the modem. So sometimes having ethics stops you from doing all the sorts of things hackers get a reputation for, because once you're being employed to look after systems and not break into them, then you have to adhere to your own code of ethics.

The other machine I hacked for that company was a dusty old SPARC box, which I rebuilt and upgraded. I picked it up and fixed it up and powered it up without thinking, and then realized I didn't have the root password for it. I asked around and no one knew what the root password was, and although I could have just switched it off and changed the password from the BOOT monitor prompt it didn't seem like a very elegant solution, nor was it going to be any fun. So I decided that I would spend a day trying to hack into this box: but in the end, it took about five minutes. This Solaris box still had its old IP address and so I could just 'rlogin' into it, and guess what? The root account on the box had a '.rhosts' file that let me log straight in without a password or anything. It just goes to show that no matter how old a security hole, people still have boxes out there which will succumb to those kinds of attacks.

A lot of computer companies and software manufacturers still haven't learnt from the early days. A certain manufacturer of high-end graphics workstations is notorious for shipping boxes out of the factory with a large number of default passwords or even null passwords, and these machines end up in the hands of incompetent systems administrators and get hacked. It's madness, but it still goes on.

ISP trojan

I used to be the main system administrator for a small British ISP, one of many which got bought up by larger companies in the Nineties. Anyway, it was a typical story of a small company, and I wasn't paid as much as I was worth on the promise of future share options and pay rises and so on and so forth. Meanwhile I watched the managing director get bigger and bigger company cars, and longer and longer business trips. So, having had enough, I moved on after a couple of years. I was rather resentful about the way the company had treated me, but I wasn't going to do anything about it.

Soon after I left, I met up with another ex-employee, and we jokingly toyed with the idea of doing something to the ISP. He mentioned that he knew my replacement's login on the main mail server, which was used by both employees and customers, and so sat outside the corporate firewall. I made a note of the details and one night, after looking at the debts I'd built up while waiting for the salary I'd been promised, I decided to have a play and see how far I could get while using a dialup account.

I was surprised to see that I could telnet into the mail server from any random IP address; indeed, there were still no IP address restrictions on it. This was an especially bad idea, as the server was running on a notoriously insecure flavour of Unix.

Anyway, after trying a few variations of the password I'd been given I successfully logged in and had user-level access. Amazed, I decided to carry on and see if I could get root. I took a few guesses at the root password, all of which failed, and decided I didn't have the knowledge to try a local exploit, or the computer power to break the encrypted password in /etc/passwd. So, necessity being the mother of invention, I wrote the worst hack ever.

First I aliased 'su' in the local user's environment to a shell script in his home directory. I then wrote the script, which was incredibly klunky, and it worked like this.

When the script was called, it displayed 'Password:' on the user's terminal just like the 'su' command, and then waited for input. Unlike the real 'su' program, it would then display the password on the user's terminal as he typed it in; but, this being such a regular task for an admin, I was hoping he wouldn't notice. The script would then write the password to a temporary file, remove the alias for the 'su' program, print to the screen that the password was incorrect – just like when the administrator has a failed password when using 'su' – and then finally delete itself.

I waited a couple of days, came back, and there was the root password.

So with the 'su' command I was in. I was root and had complete power over the mail server used by the ISP and all its customers. I had complete access to private company communications belonging to the customers, so I had access to some business plans, industry gossip and, in one noticeable case, firmware to a reasonably well-known brand of router before it was released. As far as the ISP went, its staff exchanged all their internal information via this server: so over a period of about a year, I had everything they informed each other of. They stored the passwords, in plain text, using this server, so I had access to all their routers and all the other servers. After a while spent gathering information, I could have wrecked every server they had and locked them out of it, and the same for all their routers, taking them and all their customers offline for several days. Of course, I considered doing it, but never did.

After a year I lost a lot of the information due to a hard disk crash: I hadn't backed up that much of it, and I decided that was a good sign to stop.

Script kiddies aren't all bad

When the hacker community think about script kiddies, they think about the spotty, geeky, loner teenager with a grudge against the world and something to prove. Well, this story shows that the stereotype can be very wrong and, in fact, far from the truth in many ways.

Script kiddies can do good things, and under the right circumstances they *will* do good things.

Script kiddies are not always what you think.

This is the story of an IT support person who is 25 years old, has a lot of friends, no grudges and nothing to prove to anyone. He is curious and likes to learn. He spends a lot of time commuting on the train to and from work with his head deep in a book, reading and learning all he can to quench his thirst for knowledge. His interest is computer security, computer penetration and compromise prevention.

Why do these subjects interest him? He had been a victim of hacking attacks and he took it upon himself to learn the ways of the computer underground for purely educational purposes, to ensure that he did not fall victim again.

In order to learn more about his chosen field, he dug deeper into the dark side of the web, and found himself being drawn down into the Internet underworld. Slowly, with the help of IRC, he was slowly drawn into the warez community; and this is where the story really begins.

Only five years before, this guy knew nothing about IT

other than how to work computers in a recording studio, first of all an Amiga or Atari, and then later on Macs and PCs. Only through hard work, reading, understanding and banging his head against the wall in frustration did all the hard work finally pay off. He managed to move from his position in Sales to an IT position where he could finally enjoy doing what he really loved.

He spent many late nights on IRC and FileTopia chatting to fellow computer enthusiasts with similar interests who wanted to learn, or had already learnt, about computer security in the same way that he had. The time he spent learning and practising his skills was not to go to waste, as he was soon made part of the IT security team at his corporate headquarters in a very tall building in the heart of Docklands. It was around this time that he met a group of warez dudes on IRC who opened his eyes to some of the more underground tactics used by groups to get all those mystery ftp sites and bots they have idle in their chatrooms.

Without giving too much away as to how these guys operate, let's just say that with a little help from some precompiled tools, it's so easy that a monkey could be trained to do it in exchange for a nut or a chunk of banana.

These days, peer-to-peer (P2P) networks have a bad reputation for spreading viruses, but there's a bigger threat lurking out there. Many have fallen victim to it and never knew until it was too late: the backdoor.

The victim of choice is the university or college warez freak. Of course, these guys download their warez from Napster, KaZaA, Morpheus or whatever: there are too many P2P networks to mention at times. So these warez freaks are scouring the web for copied software, and when they get the software they just load and execute the new programs they got five minutes ago.

What they don't know is that they've just executed a program which has compromised their system. A simple Trojan, one usually written from designs readily available on the web, has just installed itself on their system and allows the hacker to control the computer.

If the systems administrator is any good then no harm will be done, because the Trojan won't be able to connect to the outside world and the hacker won't be able to use the backdoor. However, if the systems administrator is over-worked, lazy or incompetent, then this will be the start of his worst nightmare.

You see, hackers – script kiddies, warez dudes, call them what you want – have organized themselves on IRC within minutes of that computer being compromised. They hang out in a secret room on IRC and go through the attack process just like a military operation: they're ready to attack the IP which has just been given them. They all know what they have to do and they use hacked proxy servers – slower computers they've already compromised – to connect to their backdoor client on the computer and attack the network.

This is the IRC warez scene at its infancy stage: these guys are n00bs[11], but though they're new to the warez scene they're still a force to be reckoned with. They have DDoS[12] bots all over the world and are really not bothered about using them against anyone who falls foul of their crew. The way they interact is like a family – a crime family – and a single unit. They're all looking out for one another, and for themselves. They welcome people who have something to

[11] *Editor's note*: This term comes from the term 'Newbie', used to describe people new to computers.
[12] *Editor's note*: DDos – 'Distributed Denial of Service' – The use of a widespread number of computer programs from many compromised hosts to overwhelm or 'deny service' by flooding a server and preventing it from performing properly.

bring to the crew: those who don't get flamed, but that's the way it goes.

One night, our friend the IT support person happened to stumble across a poorly set-up network. After a late-night, booze-fuelled session, he managed to own[13] a network server with a simple exploit[14]. He saw this as his way into the warez crew. Now that he had 10-plus ftp servers to offer, they welcomed him in with open arms: he got invited to join the forum, and much more.

It was only now that he realized there isn't really much to what warez crews do, and how they do it. They are very organized, however. They have their 'scanners' looking for systems to compromise, their 'r00ters' to compromise the systems, their backdoor creators and their 'binders': they have people to upload the software and '0-day releasers'[15] who scout for new stuff.

Now, this is where the story gets interesting. One night the IT support guy was in the IRC chatroom where the bots connected and he grabbed an IP address, thinking he'd take a look and see what it was like – nothing more. He had the client the warez group used to connect to the compromised computers they owned, so he connected and selected real-time screenshot.

The victim was using KaZaA and another P2P program which the IT support person had never seen before. He wasn't sure what it was, but he decided to investigate further.

---

[13] *Editor's note*: Own – to compromise system security at such a high level that administrator or supervisor privileges are obtained. Because the hacker can now do anything he likes with the computer, he 'owns' it.

[14] *Editor's note*: Exploit – known method of compromising system security sometimes in the form of programming code designed to take advantage of system security holes.

[15] *Editor's note*: In the warez world newer is better and best of all is '0-day warez', i.e. just cracked and released today.

It looked like IRC, but it wasn't; it just didn't work the same way. It was Windows-based, but it didn't have a name on it. Intrigued, he delved a little deeper, found the folder where the software was located and the shared folder. Normally on a P2P network such as KaZaA that'd be where the MP3s and stuff would be, so he took a look.

To his surprise, there were no MP3s, but tons of image files, short movie clips and some longer movies. Flicking back to his own PC, he decided to check out what the victim was doing before he checked the contents of the files. The victim was still running KaZaA, so the IT person zoomed into the screen to see what he was downloading.

When he realized what was going on, he recoiled in horror. This was worse than the 'Russian Execution' clip: far, far worse, because the victim was downloading child pornography. He flipped back to the shared folder, checked the contents and confirmed that he'd just found his first paedophile.

Now, the IT support person differed from most script kiddies in that he resisted the urge to send Matrix-style messages to the victim, deleting his files, and generally messing with the guy's head. Anyway, that might have alerted the victim that someone was inside the computer, but the moral dilemma for the IT support person was what he should do about what he had found.

Investigating the system further, he noted that the files were being shared with other people and were obviously coming from somewhere, so he examined the screenshots of the unknown program and noted that some of the numbers looked familiar: they were IP addresses rather than server addresses. This was eventually to be their downfall.

Should he go to the cyber cops? The police? Hacker friends? He knew what he had found was wrong but he didn't know who to turn to: after all, the police would surely want to know exactly how and why he had happened to stumble on this child pornography. He could tip off the cyber cops, but if he did that he might be traced via his own IP. He knew he could be traced, and paranoia was preventing him from doing the right thing. So what to do?

He went back to the IRC room where his friends were in the middle of flaming some hapless n00b who'd wandered in and started asking stupid questions: 'j00 d00dz w4nna sh0w me h0w 2 B l337 and B a h4x0r like u d00dz?'[16] He then immediately posted a message – 'Guys private room asap – it's mega urgent.' Once in the private 'ops only' room, everyone was asking what was going on: why the urgent meeting? He then told them about what he'd found and asked everyone what he should do.

During the animated discussion that followed, many of his friends argued the same way he had: that although they'd like to inform the cyber cops, they were worried about possible repercussions from their discovery; that because they were hacking n00bs and planting Trojans, they could get into trouble. One of the senior channel ops even went so far as to suggest that they 'do nothing' and not get involved, but this actually had the reverse effect on the group. Now they wanted to do something about it.

After a short discussion, the team decided there was only one thing they could do, and that was to plan and execute some kind of attack on these paedophiles. Scanning and probing the IP addresses of this kiddie porn ring using tools such as nmap, LANguard and SuperScanner, the warez crew soon realized most of the people were using Windows 2000 or XP.

---

[16] *Editor's note*: 'Yo dudes. Do you wanna show me how to be elite and be a hacker like you dudes?' – written as above, guaranteed flame-bait in any forum.

Being at the forefront of the computer security world meant they knew of most of the new exploits yet to be released to the general public.

This was where the fun began for this crew, because they could use their array of exploits like an arsenal of weapons by just using applications which were available to the average systems administrator. The team agreed that after permanently deleting these files simultaneously from all the computers involved, they would remote-format the hard drives on all the target machines to make sure the job was done. Then, when their task was complete, they planned to upload screenshots, logs, IP addresses and file indexes anonymously to various ftp sites and web forums with the message to spread the word and please pass the details on to the cyber cops.

Later, sitting back, the warez crew watched with a certain satisfaction as the IP addresses went down one after another, the uploads were spread across the net and the cyber cops were informed, content that what they did was right.

All except the IT support person who discovered the site in the first place – who was having second thoughts. Did he do the right thing? His online friends were hackers – they would see it the way he did, but would it have been different if he'd spoken to a 'real' person? He had so many questions, but no one to help answer them. What would you have done in this situation? Was he wrong? Could he have done anything else? And are script kiddies all that bad?

Editor's Note: It's a very bad idea to do what this person did. Apart from the fact that just looking at the child pornography was breaking the law, hacking into the servers concerned was illegal. There was no guarantee that those servers hadn't been owned in the same way as the servers the warez crew had hacked. Then the real owners wouldn't take to kindly to a group of hackers destroying their servers because of child pornography.

If anyone ever finds themselves in this situation, my advice is to inform the police, cyber or otherwise, immediately. If you're paranoid about emailing them, then send them an anonymous letter containing any supporting evidence. That way, they won't be able to trace your IP address, and they won't be able to trace you. My advice in cases like this is always, 'Leave it to the professionals.'

Novell fun

I was at college, which will remain anonymous, and I went to the admin office. There are three types of network administrator on Novell you can run into. One type of network administrator, when told that the network is insecure, will proceed to try and castrate you; another kind will say, 'Thanks very much for telling me: I'll patch it'; and the other kind does nothing and just tells you to be quiet. We had all three on our network.

The first problem I found on the Novell network was that I could write to my Novell login script – the one the administrator sets up for every user. If you write to the Novell login script it enables you to map drives and access just about anything. My excuse was that it was set up badly, so I had to rewrite it anyway.

I decided I shouldn't do what I'd done at another college, where I launched a Trojan which managed to attach itself to 51 computers in two days (but that's another story). That was the first time. I managed to get suspended for computer crime at my last college.

Basically, you could edit the login script, as well as the local user login script: the privileges for that weren't the same for the normal login script and you couldn't map drives, but who cares when you can edit the system-wide login script?

The second hole I found was a rather big one.

On the main Novell server, each username consisted of just numbers and they were mapped to a specific directory, rather like a web host; so if your username was, e.g., 20018122 it mapped into the 2001 folder, then into the 81 folder, and there would be about three or four folders in there of which 22 was one.

What they had done was map the drive to the proper area, but they still hadn't set the permissions to be able to access just that area. So theoretically you were just flipping the hierarchy button, flipping you out of that area and into the main file space on the server. You couldn't actually do that because when you flipped the hierarchy button you were booted straight into the C:\ prompt. But what you could do was to click on the drive that had been mapped and it would list on the area next to it what the specific path on the server was to your area. So it was just a matter of using Windows to cut and paste and whack it into the address bar at the top.

If you did that, you had access to everyone in the directory above you, so if it was 2001/81/22 you'd be able to access everyone else's folders in the 81 directory: full read and write permissions, everything. (It's been like this for three colleges I've been at, so I don't know if it's a problem with the administrators forgetting to set the permissions correctly or whether it's a Novell/Windows bug.) So you now have access to several users'-worth of file space to save all your dodgy script files, programs and suchlike. I even saved a copy of *Freedom Downtime* to a user's directory because I didn't want to use up all my free space.

The final and most serious bug I found was that the Novell

administration tool NWAdmin is shared. The main thing is that you're meant to be able to open it and change your own settings, but you aren't meant to be able to change other users' settings. My college was brilliant, but shall remain nameless, and Novell is so good because the administration people didn't know what they were doing.

When I opened up NWAdmin I found about half a dozen different NDS contexts, staff, admin – everything. It was the same as when checking a shell account – check you can access your own settings first – so I changed my name and made sure that worked.

The next thing I did was to search for the admin tree for the specific superuser accounts, besides the fact that they had a test account, that they called 'admin-test'.

Try guessing the password. 'Bus'? No. 'House'? No. 'Admin'? Yes, that's the one. So now we had full admin privileges anyway.

But we recently found that on Novell, when you open the administration tool, the first thing it does on a Win98 machine, which is really slow, is that it checks for permissions on the server. When I opened NWAdmin up, there were all the buttons where you change the user details for anyone in the whole tree, and that button looked like it was enabled, but when you tried to use it, it wasn't. What happens first of all is that Novell tries to check the privileges, so I ran a packet sniffer with it as well and it was sending out NCP requests to the main authentication server to actually map the rights for using this button. Doing that maps the privilege to the program, so after the splash screen goes, every single button you aren't meant to use is turned off. Somehow, by checking the rights, they've locked down the program. I immediately thought, 'This isn't going to be any help to me, because as soon as I go to do something it's going to check the privileges again and not let me do it.' So I called A___, and we decided to try something.

He whacked together a quick program which called Windows 98's APIs to find the handle of the button you were hovering over and then enable it. So, literally, you double-clicked on a user and you got the names, addresses, phone numbers and contact numbers. This is what we had access to: legitimate access, again not breaking any computer security laws. I wasn't actually violating the network agreement because the network agreement would come up the very first time you logged in from Novell to be digitally signed; but if you alt-control-delete that program and shut it down, you don't sign anything. I was logging in every time, but I wasn't signing the agreement.

You couldn't edit any of these details: you could view the other users' details, but you couldn't change them. There was an OK button in the left-hand corner: anyone who knows NWAdmin will know that the button in the corner – the OK button, the god of all buttons to change anyone's details – is disabled. So what we did was to get the little command A___ wrote, drag it on to the NWAdmin window and then enable the control for that option. It didn't have to be a button: it could have been a whole window. A lot of the frames were disabled, as well, and so we'd enable the frames.

The first thing we did was enable the Other Name text box just to check we could write to one specific user. So we added a dot in there, enabled the OK button, hit OK and it didn't check the privileges: it just wrote it to the system.

I couldn't believe this, so the next thing I tried was going into a super-user account. I didn't want to change an admin password because it would have given me away. I didn't need to log in as admin, because I already had admin privileges anyway, so who needed a proper admin login password? I had control as it was: why would I need to log in?

After this, I went to the head manager of the IT department with every other exploit we found. He was the big boss, and I told him: 'Excuse me, but you can write to the system login script', and he said 'Oh: OK. Don't tell anyone.' [17]

About a day later, once we knew we had access to these accounts, we tested the system in depth by changing the admin password. With the Change Password button that was in there, the whole frame was disabled, and you'd have to enable the frame and then enable the button, and then you'd get the dialog box to come up.

I didn't even think it would work, because surely they must check the privileges when you change the password: but no, this is Novell; they don't check privileges because they already loaded them. I don't know if this is the same for all versions of Novell, but the one we had – I think it was Novell 6.0 – again didn't check the privileges.

A few days later I was sitting in my lesson and had this tool open when the system administrator came into the room. I never hit the 'X' button as fast in my life. I thought, 'Oh, no; he's seen me.' My heart was beating like hell. But he'd only come to replace a floppy drive. He came over and replaced my floppy drive, and when I turned my computer on after he'd done it, I thought: 'I should really I tell him about this.' I wasn't sure about the reaction of one of the three system administrators: he looked like a hard man and I was pretty sure he'd try and cut my bollocks off for what I was doing.

I plucked up the courage to ask him. 'I don't know whether you know this or not, but you can access other people's areas.' I said it like that just to see what the reaction

[17] *Editor's note*: This is one of the finest examples of Security Through Obscurity I've ever heard of.

was, and it was a good reaction – 'Really?' You could see him starting to quiver.

I told him, 'First of all, you can access the system login script.' I right-clicked on Network Neighbourhood, went in there, found the right part of the network and found the login scripts. 'Look; it's enabled. You can write to it.' I actually showed him by writing a comment into the login script using the Write command, and he said, 'Oh, yes. I am aware of that: I've got to fix it.'

Then I pointed out that you could access other people's areas, and that although the drive was mapped to the right place, the permissions were set incorrectly for the level above. He started to get a bit worried now, because I hadn't finished and I'd stopped looking at him and was looking at the screen showing him all this stuff I could do.

Then I went for the main server. The mouse went over to My Computer: I double-clicked on it, loaded up, clicked on to the I:\ drive and read off the name of the main server, because I couldn't remember its name, then copied and pasted into the address bar and hit Enter.

I went into the SYSTEM directory and the systems administrator made an 'ahem'-type noise, possible bracing himself for what would follow. I then went into the PUBLIC directory and then finally the WIN32 directory, found the NWAdmin program and loaded it up. As soon as the splash screen came up, I turned round just to check how he was doing. He'd turned a shade of grey by now, as he'd seen literally the entire network map out on my screen in a window.

I knew his name, so I clicked and searched for his username using legitimate tools and, when I found it, got his login name. By now I was feeling a bit cocky and thought, 'I'll do this, purely for the fun of it.' I double-clicked on his username, found the password options, used A___'s tool to enable the frame, enabled the Change Password button, clicked on it and the dialog box came up. I turned around to look at him again and by now he was looking a shade of green.

'I'm just going to change your password to "1234",' I said, and he said, 'This is very bad: I'm glad you told me', but he didn't actually say 'Yes' or 'No' to whether I could change his password or not. I thought that must mean 'Yes', entered '1234' on both password boxes, enabled the OK button, clicked the OK button, turned to him and said, 'I've just changed your password to "1234". Next time you log in, you'll have to use that password.'

He's quivering, he's a shade of green and he says, 'I'm glad you've told me', and then 'Thank you very much for telling me: we need more people like you in our college' – and I thought, 'No, you really don't!'

Firewall follies

Never underestimate the impact of possible security vulnerability.

As an employee of an SME which was considering reselling a combined firewall and Internet server, I was invited along to a seminar by the firewall vendor. There I had the pleasure of meeting their pet pre-sales techie and ex-hacker, and we had a very long and interesting conversation about security in general, which I found rather inspiring. Especially interesting was his answer to my question, 'What does the firewall server do with email intended for a mail server it can't contact?' to which his answer was, 'I don't know.'

My girlfriend was away that weekend so I decided to have a play. I set up a lab just using my desktop and a spare firewall server box which was going to be sent to a customer in a couple of weeks. I downloaded a mail-bombing program to my desktop and bounced emails off the firewall's SMTP server just to see what would happen.

After some trial and error, I discovered that if I sent an email to an incorrect address, and from an email address which had a valid MX but couldn't be contacted, the firewall would keep the mail in its mail queue, just as it should. The email would then stay within the firewall's mail queue as it repeatedly tried to contact the mail server. The timeout for mail in the queue was three days, and this couldn't be altered within the firewall server's configuration. This problem meant that with enough email, you could fill up the firewall's mail queue.

This was a particularly bad problem because the firewall effectively had at least two mail servers, one on the outside and one on the inside. As a security measure, they used the mail queue to talk between them: a good idea, as it stopped direct communication between the outside of the firewall and the inside. But this security measure meant that if you filled this mail queue with these emails which couldn't be delivered, but had a valid MX as a destination, then the firewall stopped passing email, effectively stopping all email for the organization.

The reason this issue didn't appear to bring down the entire firewall was that the mail queue operated within its own partition, which became 101 per cent or more full, according to the disk space diagnostics, under this attack. 'A reasonably obscure and neat hack,' I thought, even if it was only a DoS attack. I therefore went to bed at some stupid time in the morning and thought nothing more of it.

However, I didn't realize quite how much service you could deny with this attack. Having had a play, and come up with a description of it for the vendor, I wiped the firewall's configuration so it could be used by the customer. The fire-wall server was duly configured to their specification and shipped to them, where it was then installed. It worked as planned, but appeared to suffer from weird behaviour and generated reasonably obscure disk space errors, complaining that partitions were full when they obviously weren't.

Realizing this was the same firewall I'd used in my lab, and that I'd only wiped the configuration rather than installing from scratch, I presumed that somehow, merely through mail-bombing the firewall server from a remote machine, I'd managed to damage its partition table in some way which was now causing all sorts of interesting problems. I was duly dispatched to reinstall the firewall from scratch. After a rein-stall, using the same hardware, all the problems went away and the firewall ran to specification.

I did attempt to phone the vendor while onsite with the customer after my reinstall fixed the problem, and I did email them details of the attack, but they never sent back more than an acknowledgement of receipt, and to this day I don't know if that firewall is still vulnerable to this attack or not.

DuffNet Systems

You know DuffNet Systems? Well, they own both FarceNet and GreedNet ISPs.

Basically I was on GreedNet first of all, and what they didn't realize is that somehow they accidentally gave every user on their ADSL network shell access to their server. It was all legitimate access. The first thing a hacker does when he gets a shell account is to check his own area to make sure he can access it. The second thing a hacker does on a shell account is to see whether he can access someone else's area. Now, I was very stupid at the time, and thought, 'OK, we'll just go and do what we need to', which was just to get a couple of big files on their server using their 'wget' commands.

About two or three days later I was on the phone to A___, who is also in our hacker clan, and we were downloading files using 'wget' commands when I suddenly thought, 'Hang on a minute: I'll just check I don't have access to other people's areas.' It was such a stupid thing: they wouldn't give you access to other people files on a shell account. It's something so stupid, it's not even an exploit: it's a misconfiguration.

So I went into the home directory, '/home1/aa', and looked for the first user I could find. 'Oh, look: he's running PHP': PHP MyAdmin, SQL configuration file. 'Oh, look: I can write, I can get files from my own space, launch script files', etc.

We were like, 'Oh, my gosh!' We were sitting on the phone laughing at how stupid they'd been. But it wasn't even that. It was even worse than that.

Now GreedNet, DuffNet, and FarceNet share the same servers. It all ran on the same server cluster: so not only did you have full access to the web space they give you for their own network: you also had access not just to GreedNet, but DuffNet and FarceNet too. By far the most popular has got to be FarceNet because if you did the List command on their networks, you had about ten pages of users.

Next, A___ had the idea of using 'ps' to list the processes running on the box, and they were using tftp – some program was using tftp; I don't know what the name of it was. The way people were connecting to the ftp server was literally the old user-colon-password[19] method, so what you got listed in the process on the Unix box was:

tftp connection, user X colon password Y[19]

OK: that lets you log in to the server, so now we can't be tracked. All right, they could log our IP address, but these guys are stupid: they can't even configure shell accounts.

We just used the password to see what was on his account. He was on DuffNet: get the login prompt, enter the username and password and find out what sort of connection this guy gets from DuffNet. This was how I found out he was using ADSL. I used to have an account on DuffNet, so I changed my ADSL dialup, used his username and password and suddenly I was logged in as him, and my static IP had changed.

Now we were completely anonymous – to a certain extent.

We got really frustrated because we wanted admin privileges: we wouldn't settle for user passwords any more, so the next thing we tried was accessing the admin directory on the Unix box. We couldn't successfully access it because it was the only thing configured properly – but that's only because it's configured properly by default.

We ran the same SSI attack we'd done on the DumbHost server, because now we had access to this guy's web space: so we uploaded this PHP script, and suddenly we found they'd misconfigured the web server to run as 'admin' on their main system. Now we had access to the admin folder on their network, so we had access to the backups of their passwords – the password hashes for just about all the users on the network. All we needed was a copy of l0phtcrack and we were away.

We didn't think it was a honey pot[20] because there were so many things wrong with it. It *couldn't* have been a honey pot, for the simple reason that they were rubbish. You have something which is a slight obstacle in a honey pot; it blocks your IP,

[18] *Editor's note*: userid:password.

[19] *Editor's note*: The process listing would show 'tftp' as the process and the userid as 'user' and the password as 'password'. This is one of the many reasons why tftp has fallen out of favour.

[20] *Editor's note*: Honeypot – a fake computer system designed to lure hackers so their techniques can be studied.

or something. To take advantage of a misconfigured shell server which gives you access – legitimate access – to people's areas isn't breaking the law because they gave you access to it.

The first rule of the Computer Misuse Act is *unauthorized access*; the second is *with intent*: if it was misconfigured incorrectly to start with, then once we were on with someone else's IP, who was going to find us?

Our static IP had changed and we were logged in using this guy's IP address. So now we had the hashed passwords for admin, and the hashed passwords for every single user on GreedNet, DuffNet and FarceNet.

They had some sort of program – I don't know its name: they were running a mounting system, and obviously had a cluster of servers, and were mounting directories on the local CGI server and directories from other servers. It was all cross-mounted without any thought for security. In the old days people used to use NFS to share directories and they'd end up sharing their entire system with the whole of the Internet, along with any old machine running NFS or PC-NFS. It was so bad that once I was on the phone to GreedNet trying to fix my ADSL and they said, 'Let me just check your log file', and I accidentally said on the phone, 'I've done that, too.'

I had a copy of the log files I'd downloaded and had looked at what it was logging. It was ironic, because the PHP script A___ made was using the URL to actually request these files, so what you'd get in the log file was 'blah blah blah dot php forward slash' and then the commands we had run – List Files, Change Directory, Remove Files, List Running Processes etc. It wouldn't have been hard for any competent admin to cop us, if we hadn't had the ability to edit and delete the log files. So we deleted all those entries. The whole network was totally and utterly insecure.

That's the other thing: there was a program running to

which we had access. We had read-and-write access via the 'vi' command on Unix, so we could be in the file and edit it while logged into the server. We downloaded a few exploits using their bandwidth – downloaded them straight to their server. We ran a port-scanner on their machine, but that was it. It got a bit bad when we were using their compilers. We used their server for about two months, but for a good four weeks it became like our machine sitting in the backdoor, which we could use now and again. They even had Lynx running, so we were using it to browse websites.

It did get to the point when we thought we were taking it too far by compiling code on their machines and editing their scripts to make the server run better, so we cut off for about a month and didn't access the server. I can't remember what it was we needed to do, but we went into the shell and GreedNet had restricted the shell accounts, so we could only access our areas. FarceNet had restricted their shell, so we could only access our area. We tried DuffNet and – yes, they've still not fixed it: so we could still access the same information through another route. It was so stupid, and they still hadn't patched the Server Side Include's vulnerability.

Denial of service

I used to run an IRC server on a large network which went through a period of being attacked quite a lot. This wasn't usually much of a problem, as I sat on the end of one of the fastest ISP networks in the UK and had well over 8Gbs of bandwidth available for the IRC server and a lot of expensive equipment behind the server to keep it up: usually, it stayed up just fine.

I kept a network analyzer handy to look at what the

données intéressantes du jour was and most attacks were quite predictable, setting ToS bits to certain values, coming from a certain range or pattern of IP addresses or attacking certain services, most of which were easily filtered by my Juniper routers.

One more interesting hack was a social-engineering hack, however.

Somebody called our support line and managed to speak to the support manager. This person told them all about IRC and how bad it was, and mentioned that some unknown person was very likely running an unauthorized IRC server on the network and that it might attract all manner of nasty attacks (of which we'd recently had many). Since I was in charge of the network, this complaint obviously went right to my desk and was filed for future use.

It was odd that most of the people who attacked the server seemed to use the network it was supporting. As much as sniffing the server would have yielded some interesting conversations, this wasn't something I was prepared to do, despite pressure from people above me in the company and law enforcement agencies. Eventually, due to the attacks and my unwillingness to snoop the server, the powers-that-be removed the IRC server from the network and that was the end of it.

Running the server had led me to develop some fairly sophisticated DoS tracking and filtering systems. The network I ran was pretty large and covered most of the world, and so I was able to trace incoming DoS attacks almost to their source. If the attack was coming from my network – and there was almost a one-in-five chance that it *was* on my network (you can work out how big my network was from that) – then I could trace it directly to the source.

Eventually, with some development, we had a network

capable of detecting a DoS attack and responding – usually before the customer who was being attacked realized what was happening. However, some more sophisticated attacks were near-impossible to filter, as they looked too much like real live data to differentiate them from – well, real live data. Take the recent WorldPay attacks, for example; they couldn't be stopped in this way.

Oddly enough, these and other attacks provided days of entertainment for my staff and me and led to the development of a leading DoS tracking system, as well as many good conversations down the pub. What they also did was to affect many other customers, some of whom had businesses depending on the Internet to survive.

I don't mind people taking stabs at my servers, and even owning them sometimes: it's usually either my own or the customer's fault for running stupidly configured systems or for being too stupid to fix security problems. When people take their silly IRC grudges out on IRC servers, run by people in their spare time because they like doing it, or when their attacks affect people who have businesses which depend on a reliable Internet connection, then I get a little pissed off at them. The thing is, I was the network engineering manager at the time. This made attacks of this nature all the more unpleasant, as the suited finger usually pointed at me.

I have a slightly different job now; the network isn't as big, but a little more cutting-edge and with a lot more customers with PCs who are more likely to be Trojaned with DoS drones; lots more people who will idle on IRC all day and get DoSed off the network as somebody tries to take over their channel. Now, I'm not saying we'll be immune to anything, but we'll be ready to sort out anything which gets thrown at us.

Afterword

Times change[21]

Times change. People change: or, more correctly, people evolve. Their needs become different and their desires shift focus. What was a demand yesterday is useless excess today; what was leading-edge then is ancient technology now. And the security industry is no different.

The security industry is very different from when I entered it, although I must give my proper respects to those who were in the scene way before I ever came around. Back then, my reasons for being were very clear to me: open and free research, education of myself and others. At the time, many others followed the same principle, and all was well.

Of course, (in)security flourished, and that means commercialization was inevitable. Granted, I don't believe your general commercial security service offering is that bad; but that's only step number one of commercialization. Once market viability was proven, then came the rush to create commodities. Security is now sold in a red box with a support contract. And this is where things went downhill.

---

[21] *Editor's note*: This afterword was taken, with permission, from www.wiretrip.net/rfp/txt/evolution.txt

I'm not the only one who feels this way. A large part of the Anti-Sec movement was based on the same cause; we just differ on the response.

Granted, it's naïve to think things will, or even can, change back to the way they were. I think that's the oversight many have. We can't go back. There are very few instances of retrograde in evolution, particularly retrograde sparked or led by a small group. And even the entire security industry would amount to a small group in the grand scheme of things.

A good example is the meaning of the term 'hacker'. At one time, it meant 'tinkerer', or someone who had an exceptional specialized skill or understanding of a subject. The subject didn't have to be security-related, or even computer-related.

Nowadays the meaning of the word is different. It has criminal connotations, largely due to media misuse. Worse, we can't change the fact that people have accepted the new meaning. But I still naïvely clung to the old meaning, and evangelized for its proper use as much as I could.

Now I realize I was in error. No one can unbrainwash the world into reclaiming the original meaning of the term. It's a dying battle; the damage has been done. The old meaning is extinct.

Except 'hacker' is not the only thing which has changed. In particular, the reasons and drives in the security research community have changed: not so much for the better or worse, but rather 'for the different'.

What was free and open research is now profit, marketing and illicit. Vendors stepped in and took control, and the Government started providing oversight. Some will say the Wild West was tamed. I say the Free West was put under lock and key.

Well, 'lock and key' is definitely extreme. It's as oppressive as you let it be, but it's hard to not feel the onerousness with all the security-related legalities which have crept up. Do the DMCA et al. really retard the 'bad guys'? After all, the DMCA is just a law, and the bad guys, by definition, are not followers of the law. They couldn't care less.

But it does have an impact on the 'good guys', particularly those like myself doing security research. It's things like the DMCA and the possibility of a misguided lawsuit at every turn which make me happy that, to this day, I have stayed behind my nym[22], as flimsy a shield as it is.

Anyway, the security industry has transgressed the parameters in which I chose to operate. Since the beginning I have always said that I'm doing what I do because I like it; it's *fun*. Well, it was fun. But it's not any more.

So now I'm left with the choice of leaving the security industry entirely, or adjusting my expectations to better fit today's snapshot of security.

This leads to the refactoring. I've decided to set new parameters for myself and how I inter-operate with the rest of the security industry. My wiretrip website is one obvious change. There are enough computer security sites and blogs on the Internet that the world doesn't need another, nor do I have any intention of doing what everyone else is doing without providing any significant unique value. Therefore I consolidated and reduced the website to the bare essentials. Superfluous material, for the sake of superfluous material, is no more.

Whisker is also no more. The demands for technical support, and the requirement to keep it updated, far outweigh the benefits of continued development. I can't compete with the commercial scanner vendors who have funds to contribute to development. I also can't compete with large projects, which have many hands to help maintain code bases.

[22] *Editor's note*: nym – pseudonym or handle designed to protect a hacker.

This doesn't even take into account the general futility of CGI scanning in this day and age. So it's done.

Also done are my speaking engagements. I don't plan on answering any more CFPs or accepting any more invitations. I don't have anything left to speak about, nor anything I wish to speak of which would benefit anyone other than curious researchers. I'm going to enjoy being in the crowd for once.

I've had a lot of good moments in the past few years in this industry, and I'm sure there's still a few more to be had. I will still be around, my research will still continue and development of Libwhisker will still happen. But the days of free security research for the sake of free security research are numbered, if not completely over already.

Don't lose sight of security. Security is a state of being, not a state of budget. He with the most firewalls still does not win. Put down that honey pot and keep up-to-date with your patches. Demand better security from vendors and hold them responsible. Use what you have, and make sure you know how to use it properly and effectively.

And above all else, don't abuse or take for granted sources of help and information. Without them, you might find yourself lost or inconvenienced.